THE KIDS CAN PRESS JUMBO BOOK OF MUSIC

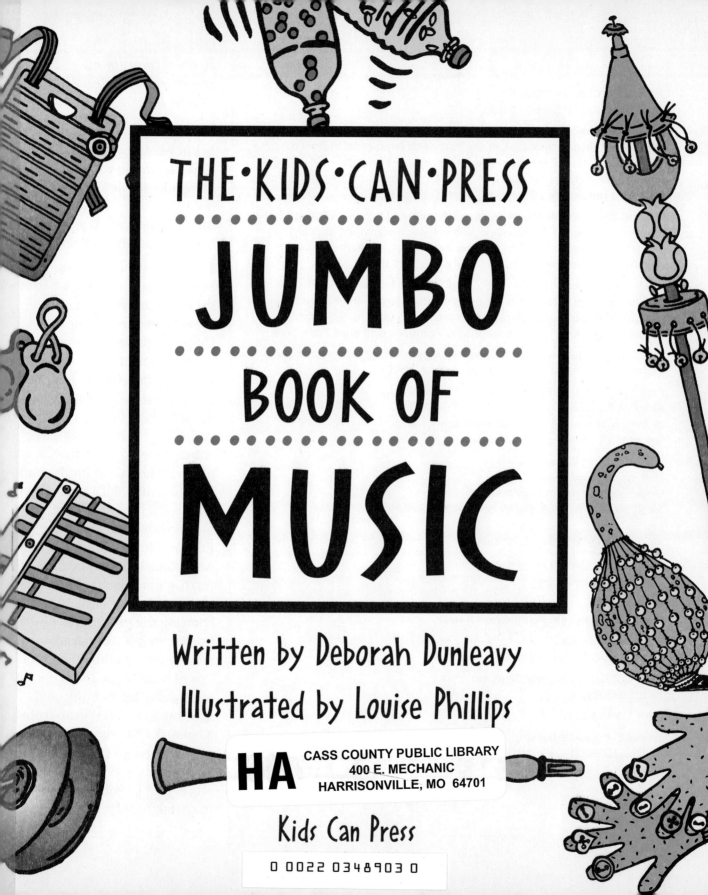

THE·KIDS·CAN·PRESS
JUMBO
BOOK OF
MUSIC

Written by Deborah Dunleavy

Illustrated by Louise Phillips

Kids Can Press

Kids Can Press acknowledges the financial support of the Government of Canada, through the BPIDP, for our publishing activity.

Published in Canada by
Kids Can Press Ltd.
29 Birch Avenue
Toronto, ON M4V 1E2

Published in the U.S. by
Kids Can Press Ltd.
2250 Military Road
Tonawanda, NY 14150

Edited by Linda Biesenthal
Designed by Karen Powers
Model photography by Ray Boudreau
Music instrument photography by Frank Baldassarra

Music notation by Howard Alexander

Printed and bound in Canada

CM PA 01 0 9 8 7 6 5 4 3 2 1

Canadian Cataloguing in Publication Data

Dunleavy, Deborah
      The jumbo book of music

(The Kids Can Press jumbo book series)
Includes index.

ISBN 1-55074-723-1

1. Music — Juvenile literature. 2. Musical instruments — Juvenile literature. I. Phillips, Louise. II. Title. III. Series: Kids Can Press jumbo book series.

MT740.D922 2001   j780   C00-931790-2

Kids Can Press is a Nelvana company

Dedication

To the memory of my grandmother, Bertha Wylie, who let me play her guitar when I was a child.

Acknowledgments

A special thank you to Howard Alexander for doing the music notation, for explaining how music sometimes works and for his constant encouragement.

Thanks to Lance Besharah for helping out with the tin-can steel drums; to my editor, Linda Biesenthal, for sharing and shaping the vision for this book; to gong master David Bullock, who lives in Australia and helped me understand how gongs work; to Cathy Fink for her expertise on yodelling; to David Hain, who showed me how bagpipes work; to Peter Hutchison for drumming tips; to Orma McDougall, who taught me how much fun barbershop singing can be; to Edward Moll for lending a hand with some of the more difficult instruments, like the thumb piano; to Louise Phillips for showing the playfulness of the book with her wonderful illustrations; to Bill Russell for lots of song ideas; to Katherine Smitherine for listening and sharing; to Karen Wilson from New York City who taught me "Chawe Chidyo Chem'Chero"; and to the Brockville Public Library for providing resource material from far and wide.

CONTENTS

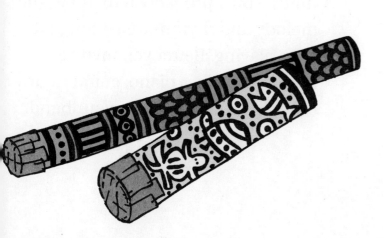

OPENING NOTE

This book is all about making music — with homemade instruments, with your voice, your hands, your feet and lots of other body parts. Best of all, it's about putting a band together and making music with your friends.

Each chapter features a different kind of band. There's something for everyone's musical taste. If you like the sound of steel drums and bongos, check out the Carnival Band. Try the String Band if guitar and fiddle music is more your style. Head straight for the World Beat Band if you love the haunting drone of a didgeridoo. Try the A Cappella Jam Band if you and your friends want to create a great jazz sound using just your voices. And if you're a solo performer, the One Kid Band is for you.

Inside each chapter are instructions for making a variety of instruments. You'll also find tips on how to play them and ideas for putting them together to create a great band sound. You'll even find the words and music for two band songs. Most are familiar tunes that you've probably heard hundreds of times. You should be able to play these songs using your ears instead of the music notes. But don't be afraid to try a song that isn't so familiar. Ask someone who reads music to play it for you. After hearing it just a few times, you'll probably remember the melody and rhythm well enough to start playing. Better yet, invite a friend who plays piano, guitar or any other instrument to join your band.

But don't stop there! Once you've tried the bands in this book — get creative. Mix and match homemade instruments from different chapters — as well as homemade instruments with the standard store-bought variety — to create a band with its own unique sound. Then make up some of your own rhythms and tunes. You'll find some ideas to get you started composing songs in the Trash Band chapter. And in the Marching Band chapter, you'll find tips on how to conduct a band so it sounds just the way you want it to.

Here's some advice — from one musician to another: Always trust your ears when you're playing. If it sounds good, you're making music!

MAKING INSTRUMENTS

The first string instrument was probably invented more than 30 000 years ago when hunters — who had a bit of time on their hands — started plucking away on the sinew strung on their hunting bows. Before long, they discovered that if they loosened the sinew by bending the bow, their plucking produced a different note.

Another ancient musician invented one of the first wind instruments by turning a hollow animal bone into a flute. Even Stone Age flutes had at least one finger hole, so somebody had figured out that the bone-with-a-hole produced one note when the hole was covered and a different note when it was uncovered.

GONG! GONG!

GONG GONG!

With a bit of practice and a good ear, these musicians learned to produce a full range of musical sounds playing simple instruments made from things they had on hand. And so will you!

You'll find most of the things you need to make the instruments in this book lying around the house or in the recycling bin. As you're hunting and gathering instrument parts, keep your eyes open for other things that produce interesting sounds. Anything that you can hit, scrape, rattle, shake, blow, buzz, pluck or strum can be turned into a musical instrument. Even the kitchen sink!

A note of caution!

Some of the tools you'll be using to make the instruments in this book are sharp and pointy. Be very careful when handling them. Stay on the safe side and ask an adult to help — especially when using a drill or craft knife. Use lots of duct tape to cover any rough ends or edges. If your finished instruments look less than cool, just decorate them with your favorite colors and designs.

All in the Family

Most musicians, bands and orchestras divide instruments into three families — percussion, wind and string. These families will help you put instruments together when you're organizing your band. But there's also the Hornbostel and Sachs way of classifying instruments. It divides them into four families, based on how musical sounds are produced. Keep these families in mind when you're making your instruments.

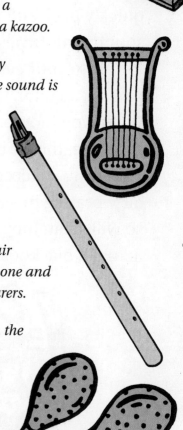

● *The membranophone family includes instruments whose sound is produced by a vibrating skin, or membrane. A kettledrum is a membranophone and so is a kazoo.*

● *The chordophone family includes instruments whose sound is produced by vibrating strings. A piano is a chordophone and so is a one-stringed mouth bow.*

● *The aerophone family includes instruments that produce sound by making air vibrate. A flute is an aerophone and so are whistles and bull-roarers.*

● *In the idiophone family, the instruments themselves produce vibrations. Gongs and cymbals are iodiophones and so are steel drums and maracas.*

THE SOUNDS OF MUSIC

So what's the difference between a musical sound that makes you tap your toes and a horrible noise that makes you cover your ears? It's all a matter of vibrations.

Anything that vibrates, or moves quickly back and forth, creates a sound that travels in a wave through the air to your ear. When you're playing a guitar, the string vibrates. When you blow across the mouthpiece of a flute, the air inside the flute's tube vibrates. A screechy scream will set the air vibrating in a different way — and so will scratching your fingernails across a blackboard!

The vibrations of cover-your-ears noises are all jagged and jumbled. They look pretty scary, something like this:

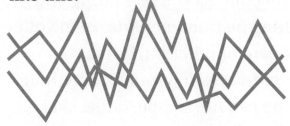

The vibrations of a perfectly plucked guitar string look a lot more calm, cool and collected. That's because they are regular and fall into a pattern, something like this:

✳ A VARIETY OF VIBRATIONS

That perfectly plucked guitar string produces just one note. So how do guitar players get so many different musical sounds or notes from each string?

Here are a few clues: the smaller, shorter or tighter something is, the faster it vibrates, and the faster the vibrations, the higher the sound. And then there's vice versa: the bigger, longer or looser something is, the slower it vibrates, and the slower the vibrations, the lower the sound.

It's easy to test this out. Wrap a rubber band around the open side of the bottom part of a shoebox. Pluck the band and listen to the sound of the note. Now, press a finger on the band near one end of the box. Pluck and listen. Keep moving your finger further along the band and keep plucking. Each time you press the band you're making it shorter and producing a higher note.

It's the same thing with instruments that you blow — except that you're changing the length of a column of air instead of a string. When a flute player covers a finger hole, the column of air gets longer because the air can't escape through the hole. A longer column slows down the vibrating air and produces a lower note.

Your band needs string and wind instruments that produce different notes in order to play melodies and harmony. But your band also needs a drum or other percussion instruments. It's their job to help you play a pattern of one-note, toe-tapping, finger-snapping beats. If you've got that, you've got rhythm. And that's the heart and soul of music!

Now let the music begin!

ONE KID BAND

Get ready to make your own ankle rattlers, button gloves and broiler-tray frattoire. When your instruments are made, it's show time. Bong your gong! Whirl your whirlies! Shake your rattler! In this band, you are conductor and orchestra all in one.

* Make a musical hat
* Play a whistle collar
* Presenting ... the One Kid Band Musical Show!

♫ MUSIC NOTES

Am I Making Music Yet?

To make music, you need beat and rhythm. A beat is a steady pulse. When you put beats together in a pattern that gets repeated, you've got rhythm.

Your heart has a steady pulse when it's pumping blood through your body. You can feel your own heartbeats by touching the inside of your wrist. Try tapping your toes to your heartbeat.

In your One Kid Band, you'll know you're making music when you hear a regular pattern of toe-tapping, hand-clapping beats.

Musical Hat

Who says you don't use your head to play music? With this musical topper, you can entertain a crowd — not to mention yourself — for hours. It keeps the rain off, too!

★ WHAT YOU NEED

plastic baseball helmet

drill

pot lid

screwdriver

nut and bolt

bicycle horn

reflector lights and decals

★ How You Make It

1 Ask an adult to help you drill two holes in the helmet — one on top for the gong and one on the side of the visor.

2 Remove the screw that holds the knob to the pot lid. Screw the lid to the baseball helmet so that it's upside down on top of the helmet and the knob is inside.

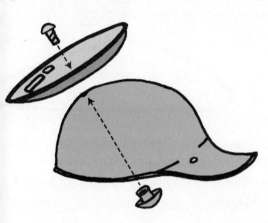

3 Use the nut and bolt to attach the horn to the front of the helmet.

4 For decoration, you can add reflector lights and decals.

★ How You Play It

Clang your pot-lid gong with a wooden spoon. Beat out a rat-a-tat rhythm on your musical hat and honk the horn. Try this familiar tune:

Found a peanut,
(clang)

Found a peanut,
(clang)

Found a peanut last night.
(clang, clang)

Last night
(rat-a-tat-tat)

I found a peanut,
(clang)

Found a peanut
(clang)

Last night.
(honk)

Whistle Collar

Make a whistle collar so that you can play kazoo, whistle and whirlie at will. You'll find a whirlie in toy or music stores. It's a round whistle that makes a whirling sound — wheee!

coat hanger

wire cutters

packing tape

picture wire

whistle

kazoo

whirlie

* HOW YOU MAKE IT

1 Use wire cutters to remove the hook from the coat hanger. Wrap tape around the twisted ends of the coat hanger.

2 Bend the coat hanger into a more rounded shape and try it on. It should sit comfortably on your shoulders. Remove and place on your worktable.

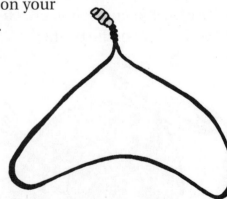

3 For each instrument, cut 30 cm (12 in.) of picture wire. Crisscross the wire around each instrument and the coat hanger, attaching the instruments to the front of the collar about 5 cm (2 in.) apart. The mouthpieces should face inward.

4 Wrap tape over the wire to keep the instruments from slipping around the hanger.

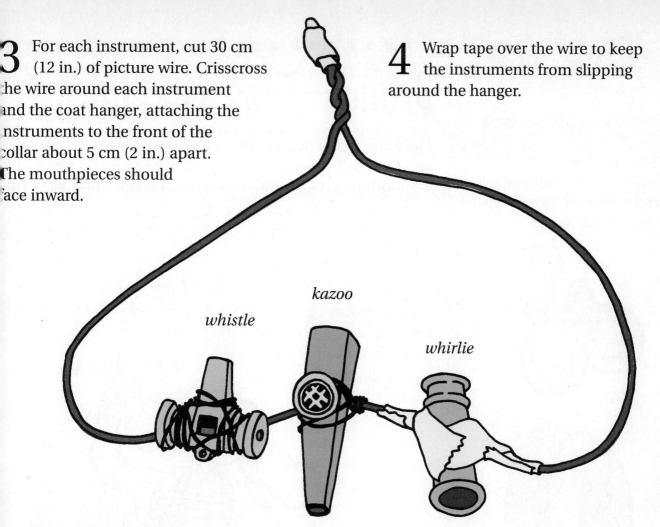

kazoo

whistle

whirlie

★ How You Play It

Put on your whistle collar and practice playing each instrument without using your hands. Then try playing "Shave and a haircut." To start, say "too, too-too, too, too" into your kazoo. At the end, blow your whistle and your whirlie.

Beats	1	2	3	4	1	2	3	4
	Shave	**and a**	**hair-**	**cut,**	**—**	**two**	**bits**	**—**
	Too	*too-too*	*too*	*too*		*tweet*	*whee!*	
	(Kazoo)					(whistle)	(whirlie)	

♪ MUSIC NOTES

Percussion Instruments

Percussion instruments are musical instruments that you scrape, shake or hit with your hands or a beater.

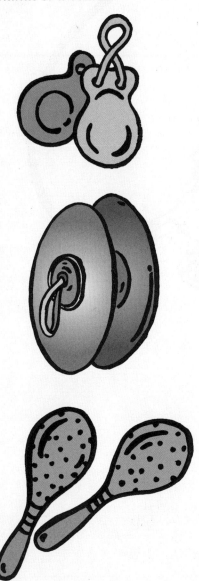

Broiler-Tray Frattoire

The frattoire is a popular percussion instrument played mostly by folk musicians in the southern United States. It is a rub board made out of a sheet of metal with ridges on it. To make a loud, raspy rhythm, musicians hang it over their shoulders and rub spoons or thimbles up and down the ridges.

A broiler tray — that bumpy metal thing that lives in your oven — makes a great frattoire. You can also use a paint tray that has ribs on the bottom. Play your frattoire with spoons, thimbles on your fingers or button gloves (page 22).

✴ What You Need

broiler tray

bicycle bell

2 narrow belts

✴ How You Make It

1 Attach the bicycle bell through a hole to the side and near the top of the broiler tray.

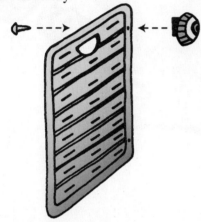

2 Slip one belt through the slit on the top right of the broiler tray and the other belt through the slit on the top left. Fasten each belt.

✴ How You Play It

Slip your arms through the belt loops so that the broiler tray hangs on your chest. Rub, tap and scrape the spoons across the ribs of the tray. Practice by moving one spoon up and down the tray. Try the other spoon. Then rub with both spoons, so that one rubs up while the other rubs down. It should feel as natural as swinging your arms when you walk.

✴ Frattoire Practice

You can play one spoon at a time like this:

Beat	1	2	3	4
Right hand	down		down	
Left hand		down		down

You can rub up and down. While one hand rubs down, the other rubs up.

Beat	1	2	3	4
Right hand	down	up	down	up
Left hand	up	down	up	down

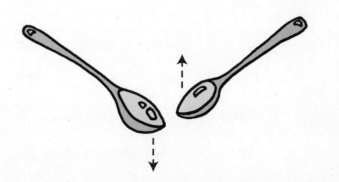

Button Gloves

When you wear your button gloves, your fingers get to tap dance on your frattoire.

These are really easy to make. Find an old pair of cotton or wool gloves and eight buttons, one for each finger (thumbs don't count). Using needle and thread, sew a button on the pad of each fingertip of the gloves. Put them on and let your fingers fly up and down your frattoire.

* MORE FRATTOIRE PRACTICE

You're wearing your button gloves and frattoire. Now don your musical hat, and add some pot-lid clangs and bicycle-bell rings to your frattoire practice.

Beats	1	2	3	4	1	2	3	4
The	**old**	**gray**	**mare**	**she**	**ain't**	**what she**	**used to**	**be,**
Rub	*rub*	*rub*	*rub*	*rub*			*clang*
	Ain't	**what she**	**used to**	**be,**	**ain't**	**what she**	**used to**	**be.**
Rub			*clang*	*rub*			*clang*
The	**old**	**gray**	**mare**	**she**	**ain't**	**what she**	**used to**	**be**
Rub	*rub*	*rub*	*rub*	*rub*			*clang*
	Many	**long**	**years —**	**a -**	**go.** ————————————————————————
Rub ————	*(keep rubbing fast)*		————————————————————				*ring!*

Ankle Rattler

Rattles worn on ankles. Rattles worn on wrists. Rattles worn on necks, and rattles worn on hips. When you wear a rattle, it moves when you move. If you are dancing, the rattles jingle with each step. The light, tinkling sound rises above the lower sounds of your other One Kid Band instruments.

* WHAT YOU NEED

elastic 4 cm (1½ in.) wide and 20 cm (8 in.) long

scissors

6 jingle bells

needle and thread

* HOW YOU MAKE IT

1   Cut a length of elastic to fit loosely around your ankle (or wrist). Be sure it's long enough to be pulled on over your foot (or hand).

2   Sew the bells onto the elastic band, spacing them evenly apart.

3   Sew the two ends of the elastic together using small stitches so that they hold firmly.

* HOW YOU PLAY IT

Put your rattler on an ankle or wrist. Listen to the bells as you move. See what kind of beat patterns (or rhythm) you can make.

One Kid Band Musical Show

Here's where you get to gong the pot lid on your musical hat, blow your whirlie, jingle your ankle rattler, honk your horn, ring your bike bell and rub your frattoire.

When you are all set up in your musical attire, it's time to grab the spotlight and dazzle your friends and folks with your musical talent.

STOMP! GONG·GONG!

✳ WARMING UP

Before stepping onto the stage, practice using foot stomps and your musical-hat gong:

Beats	1	2	3	4	5	6	7	8
	Left foot	*right foot*	*left foot*	*right foot*	Gong	*gong*	*gong*	*(rest)*

Keep playing this pattern of beats until you feel comfortable with it. Start slowly and gradually move on to a faster speed.

✷ It's Show Time!

Pick an easy tune to start with, such as "Row, Row, Row Your Boat." Rub your button gloves, thimbles or spoons up and down your frattoire while humming the song into the kazoo on your whistle collar. At the end of each line, add another instrument for a special musical effect.

Beats	①	②	③	④	①	②	③	④
Row,	**row,**	**row**	**your boat**	**Gently**	**down the**	**stream,**	————
Gong	*gong*	*gong*	*(rest)*	*(rest)*	*(rest)*	*(rest)*	*whirlie*
Merrily,	**merrily,**	**merrily,**	**merrily**	**Life is**	**but a**	**dream.**	————
Jingle	*jingle*	*jingle*	*jingle*	*Honk!*	*(rest)*	*(rest)*	*Rub loudly and end with a huge gong CRASH!*

Aikendrum

This silly fellow is made up of all kinds of meat, fruit and vegetables and usually plays upon a large spoon called a ladle. You can play upon any number of your One Kid Band instruments.

1. There was a man lived in the moon, in the moon, in the moon, there was a man lived in the moon and his name was Ai - ken - drum.
2. He played up - on a rub — board, rub — board, rub — board, he played up - on a rub — board and his name was Ai - ken - drum.

3. His eyes were made of meatballs, meatballs, meatballs,
   His eyes were made of meatballs and his name was Aikendrum.

4. He played upon a head gong, head gong, head gong,
   He played upon a head gong and his name was Aikendrum.

5. His hair was made of spaghetti, spaghetti, spaghetti,
   His hair was made of spaghetti and his name was Aikendrum.

6. He played upon a rattler, rattler, rattler,
   He played upon a rattler and his name was Aikendrum.

Turkey in the Straw

Enjoy your favorite frattoire rhythms with this
upbeat song. Play a few of your One Kid Band
instruments as a chorus. Don't sing the words,
just play the rhythm of them.

Well I had a lit-tle chick-en and it would-n't lay an egg. So I

poured hot wat-er up and down its leg. Well the lit-tle chick-en cried and the

lit-le chick-en begged and the sil-ly old chick-en laid a hard boiled egg.

Turk-ey in the straw, haw, haw, haw, turk-ey in the hay, hay, hay, hay. The

old folks danced with their moth-er-in-law as they

played a lit-tle tune called "Turk-ey in the Straw."

MARCHING BAND

Strike up the band! Beat your big bass drum. Tap your tin tambourine. Blast away on a rubber-hose bugle. Bring on the baton twirlers and the dancing clowns. Parade right through your neighborhood with your very own Marching Band.

* Practice drumrolls
* Make your own panpipes
* Conduct a Marching Band

The March King

John Philip Sousa started playing in the United States Marine Band in 1867, when he was only 13. At 26, he was promoted to bandmaster. In 1892, he formed Sousa's Band, which played popular concerts across North America and Europe. Sousa composed more than 100 marches, including "The Stars and Stripes Forever." To this day, he is known as the March King.

MARCHING MUSIC

Music for marching has a strong beat to help large groups of people keep in step and move together. This came in handy on the battlefields of long ago when soldiers had to march in formation to face the enemy. By the middle of the 1600s, marching bands were also leading religious processions and celebrating a king's arrival in town. Marches became so popular that, in the 1800s, even serious composers were writing them.

Marching Beats

The beat of the drum keeps a parade or procession moving. Some marching rhythms follow a pattern of two beats. The first beat is the strongest: **one** two, **one** two. This stress, or accent, on the first beat keeps everyone in step. "Yankee Doodle" has a two-beat marching rhythm pattern.

First, march and count out the beat. Then sing the song as you march.

Count	1	2	3	4	1	2	3	4
March	*Left*	*right*	*left*	*right*	*left*	*right*	*left*	*right*
Sing	**Yank - ee**	**doodle**	**went to**	**town**	**rid - ing**	**on a**	**po -**	**ny**

Other marches have a pattern of four beats. The stress can fall on the first and third beats or just on the first beat. Try this out:

Count	1	2	3	4	1	2	3	4
March	*Left*	*right*	*left*	*right*	*left*	*right*	*left*	*right*
Sing	**Glo -**	**ry,**	**glo - ry,**	**Hall - e -**	**lu -**	——	**jah!**	——

DRUM RHYTHMS

In a marching band, the drum beats out the rhythm. You can beat out drum rhythms on any surface — on the top of a thick phone book or on the bottom of a wastebasket. Two wooden spoons or chopsticks make fine drumsticks.

Sticks and Grips

You'll get a different sound or tone from your drum if you use different materials for your drumsticks. Try knitting needles, thick dowels or pencils. Some will sound soft or muted. Others will sound hard or crisp. Experiment with different knobs for your drumsticks, too — metal nuts, sponges, wooden beads, bottle corks, rubber balls or wool.

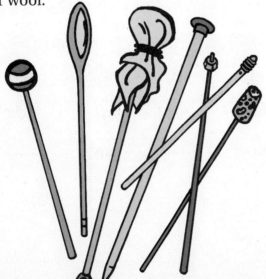

There are two ways of holding a drumstick.

*The traditional marching grip is called the **rabbit grip**.*

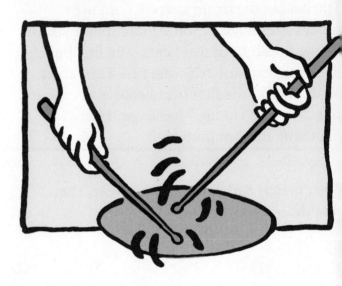

*The other way of holding a drumstick is called the **matched grip**.*

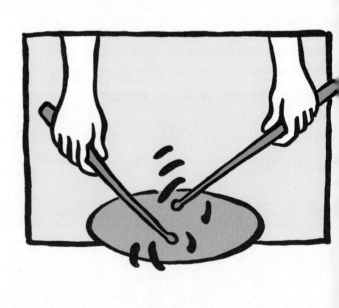

Left, Right, Left, Right

Beat your drumming surface first with the left stick (L), then with the right stick (R). The shaded squares indicate the strongest (stressed) beats.

L R L R L R L R

Practice keeping the beats steady. Start slowly and then pick up the tempo (speed) of your beats by drumming faster.

Drum Rolls

According to the National Rudimental Drummers Association, you can make 13 different rhythms with drumsticks. These rhythms have names, and some of the names copy the sounds the drumsticks make. Here are a few. Say the word slowly and then fast as you beat out its rhythm. Use both your right (R) and left (L) drumsticks.

Paradiddle:

L R L L

Or try:

R L R R

Ratamacue:

L L L R

Or try:

R R R L

Practice doing drumrolls using other words:

Gum: quick R

Ju-jube: quick R L

Jelly bean: R R L

Licorice stick: R L R L

Water-Cooler Bass Drum

For your parade, you'll want to hit a loud bass drum to keep the marchers in step. A recycled water-cooler jug makes a big, booming sound when struck with a drumstick or beater.

✳ What You Need

18 L (5 U.S. gal.) empty water-cooler jug

thick knitting needle

small rubber ball

✳ How You Make It

1 Stick the small rubber ball onto the end of the thick knitting needle to make a beater.

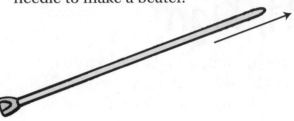

2 Hold the jug under one arm and strike the bottom and sides with the drumstick beater.

⭐ How You Play It

For a marching beat, hit the bottom harder than the side:

bottom   side   **bottom**   side   **bottom**   side   **bottom**   side

Try hitting just the bottom following this accented rhythm pattern. Hit harder on the bold beats.

Count	1	2	3	4	1	2	3	4
	Boom	*Bah*	**Boom**	*Bah*	**Boom**	*Bah*	**Bah**	*(rest)*
	Boom	*Bah*	**Boom**	*Bah*	**Boom**	*Bah*	**Bah**	*(rest)*

⭐ Forward, March!

Make up your own march using your bass drum. Here's one to try:

Walk the dog *(boom, boom)*

To the park *(boom, boom),*

Better get back *(boom, boom)*

Before it's dark *(boom, boom).*

Tin Tambourine

Every marching band needs the rattle and tap of a tambourine! A tambourine is just a flat metal frame with rattles attached to it. Here's how to make your own version of this percussion instrument.

* What You Need

scrap of wood

16 metal bottle caps

metal cake tin or pie plate

hammer

large nail

twine

* How You Make It

1 Use the scrap piece of wood to protect the table you are working on. Place cap ridges down on the wood. Use the hammer and nail to punch a hole in the center of each cap.

2 Use the hammer and nail to punch eight evenly spaced holes around the sides of the cake tin (or the rim of the pie plate).

3 Cut eight lengths of twine, each one about 20 cm (8 in.) long.

4 Tie a knot at one end of a piece of twine. Thread two caps back to back onto the twine.

5 Slip the twine through a hole in the cake tin. Make a knot inside.

6 Repeat until all the caps are tied to the cake tin.

✷ How You Play It

Hold the tambourine in one hand and tap the center with your other hand. Now tap near the edge. You can also shake the tambourine or hit it against your hip. Try these rhythm patterns. Hit harder on the bold beats.

① **2** **①** **2** **①** **2** **①** **2**

Hip tap **hip** tap **hip** tap **hip** tap

Tap shake **tap** hip **tap** tap **shake** shake

✷ Shake, Shake!

Shake it up when it's your turn to take out the trash:

See this trash
(shake, shake),

So much waste
(shake, shake),

Too much junk
(shake, shake)

All over the place
(shake, shake).

♫ MUSIC NOTES

Tube Trombone

You can make your own tube trombone by fitting one piece of tubing into another. Blast away into the smaller tube and use the larger one as the slide. Remember: the longer the tube, the lower the note.

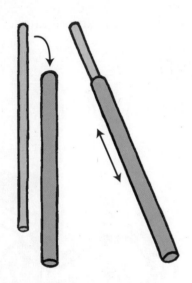

♫ SOUND BITES

Bugle Calls

In military camps, buglers play "taps" when it's time for lights out and "reveille" when it's time for rise and shine. Try your own bugle calls — but warn the family first!

BRASS INSTRUMENTS

Large military bands include brass wind instruments — tubas, trumpets, French horns and trombones. Each of these instruments has a tube that flares out at the end. Trumpets, French horns and tubas have valves that help to change the pitch of the notes (how high or low the notes are). When the valve is pressed down, the tubing gets longer. The longer the tube, the lower the note.

Blast Away!

Collect different kinds of tubes — a piece of garden hose, copper pipe or cardboard tubing. The tube needs to be small enough in diameter so you can seal the end closed with your mouth.

To make a buzzing sound, smile with your lips closed. Blow out air so that your lips vibrate.

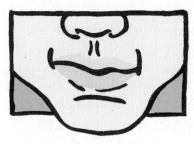

Now hold the tube up to your lips and blast into it.

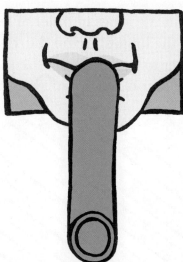

To change the pitch of your notes, change your lips. The looser your lips, the lower the note.

Rubber-Hose Bugle

This bugle isn't made out of brass, but it's great for blasting out some marching rhythms.

✳ What You Need

1 L (1 qt.) plastic pop bottle

scissors or craft knife

piece of rubber hose 60 cm (2 ft.) long

masking tape

✳ How You Make It

1 Cut off the top of the plastic pop bottle, about 10 cm (4 in.) down from the spout. Now you have a funnel-shaped end for your horn.

2 Insert the hose into the spout of the funnel. Secure with tape. Wrap more tape around the joint — where the funnel meets the hose.

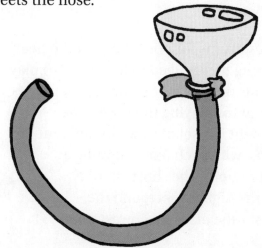

Plastic-Tube Panpipes

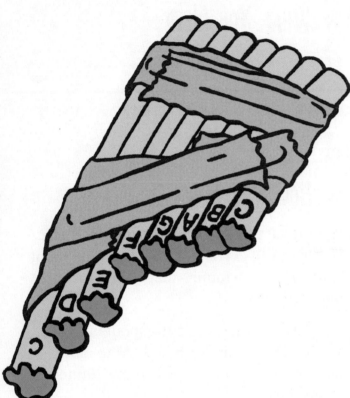

Besides drums for pounding out the beat, marching bands need instruments to play the tune, or melody, of a march. Panpipes are great for playing the tune. This intrument is a set of tubes of different lengths, with each one sounding a different note. The shortest tube plays the highest note, and the longest tube plays the lowest note.

✳ WHAT YOU NEED

about 1.2 m (4 ft.) of plastic tubing, 1 cm (½ in.) in diameter

ruler

color marker

knife

packing tape

4 ice cream sticks

plasticine

✳ HOW YOU MAKE THEM

1 Measure and mark these lengths on the tubing. Cut with a sharp knife. (Ask an adult to help.) The letters indicate notes.

C = 17.5 cm (7 in.)   **G** = 12 cm (4¾ in.)
D = 16.5 cm (6½ in.)   **A** = 10.5 cm (4¼ in.)
E = 14.5 cm (5¾ in.)   **B** = 10 cm (4 in.)
F = 13.2 cm (5¼ in.)   **C** = 9.4 cm (3¾ in.)

2 Lay out the tubes in order of length from the longest to the shortest. Use your marker to write the note letter on each pipe.

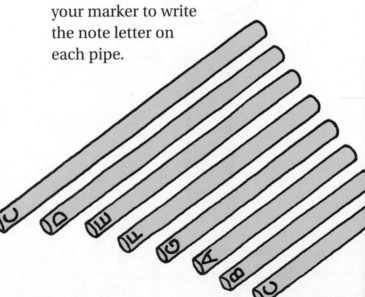

3 Pair up the tubes: **C** and **D**, **E** and **F**, **G** and **A**, **B** and **C**. Tape the pairs together at the bottom and top.

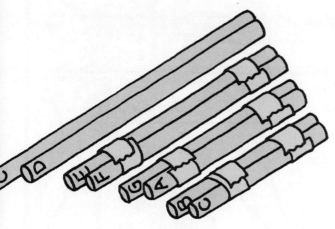

5 Place one ice cream stick along the top and another one along the bottom of one side. Hold in place with tape. Turn the pipes over and tape two more ice cream sticks to the pipes, lining them up with the first two sticks. Secure the sticks with tape wrapped around the pipes.

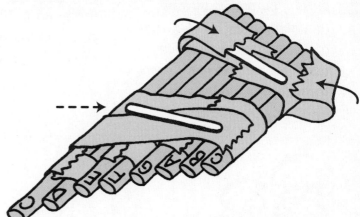
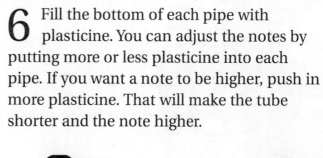

4 Tape all four pairs together. Keep the openings at the tops level for easy playing.

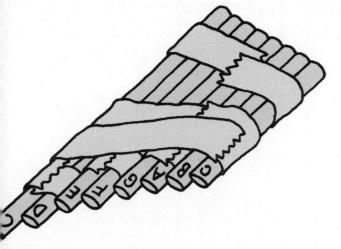

6 Fill the bottom of each pipe with plasticine. You can adjust the notes by putting more or less plasticine into each pipe. If you want a note to be higher, push in more plasticine. That will make the tube shorter and the note higher.

🎼 Sound Bites

Marching Panpipers!

In the early 1800s, panpipe bands were very popular in parts of Europe. Musicians tucked panpipes into the front of their jackets so that their hands were free to play drums, triangles and tambourines.

✳ How You Play Them

Hold the pipes so that the top of the instrument is just below your lips and the bottom points to the floor. Blow gently across the top of the tubes.

✳ Panpipe Practice

Try this version of "Yankee Doodle" on your panpipes. This song has a note that is a little higher than F and a little lower than G. It is called F-sharp (F#). You will need another pipe for F#. Cut a tube 12.5 (5 in.) long. Fill the end with plasticine and tape it on top of your panpipes between F and G.

1		2		1		2	
G	G	A	B	G	B	A——	
G	G	A	B	G——		F#——	
G	G	A	B	C	B	A——	
F#	D	E	F#	G——		G——	

Johnny Jingle

The leader of a marching band usually carries a baton, and it waves up and down to the beat while the band parades through the street. The Johnny Jingle, sometimes called the Turkish Crescent, is a fancy rattle that was used by Turkish military bands.

The Johnny Jingle is a perfect instrument for the leader of the band. While marching, hit the bottom of the Johnny Jingle on the floor or ground and the bells will help keep the rhythm.

* WHAT YOU NEED

dowel about 2 cm thick and 1 m long (¾ in. x 39 in.)

drill

screwdriver

spring-type door stopper

hammer

7 nails 4 cm (1½ in.) long

large nail or spike

small tuna or cat food can, top removed

twine

about 26 bells of various sizes

sharp craft knife

2 tennis balls

white glue

4 pieces of cardboard 25 cm x 25 cm (10 in. x 10 in.)

plastic funnel 10 cm (4 in.) in diameter

bottle cap

* HOW YOU MAKE IT

1 With adult help, drill a hole in the bottom of the dowel. Use the drill bit that is slightly smaller than the screw for the door stopper. Use a screwdriver to attach the door stopper to the bottom of the dowel.

2 Measure 30 cm (12 in.) down from the top of the dowel. Mark four spots at this length, equal distances apart, around the dowel. Hammer a nail into the dowel at each spot.

3 Use the hammer and large nail to pierce 10 holes about 2.5 cm (1 in.) apart around the tuna can.

4 Cut ten 20-cm (8-in.) lengths of twine. String a bell onto each piece of twine and tie the bells to the can.

5 In the center of the can, make a hole large enough so that the can fits onto the dowel. Be careful with the sharp edges. Slide the can down the dowel until it rests on the nails.

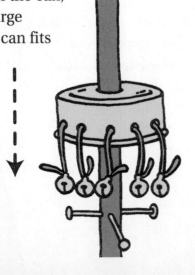

6 To hold the tennis balls in place, hammer a nail into each side of the dowel about 2.5 cm (1 in.) above the tuna can.

7 Cut an X into the top and bottom of each tennis ball. Insert 2 bells into each ball. Push the balls onto the nails.

8 Glue the four pieces of cardboard together. Let them dry. Draw a crescent shape on the cardboard. Make the open end no wider than the inside diameter of the funnel. Cut out the crescent.

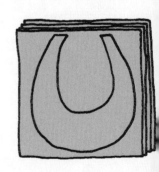

9 Use a pencil to make a hole up through the center of the cardboard layers. Slip the crescent onto the dowel.

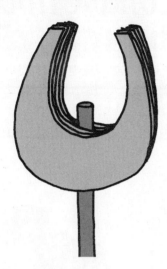

10 With the nail, punch eight holes, evenly spaced, around the outside rim of the funnel. Thread eight bells onto eight lengths of twine and attach them to the funnel.

11 Place the funnel on the dowel so that the ends of the crescent are tucked inside the funnel.

12 Hammer a nail through the center of a bottle cap. Hammer the bottle cap to the top of the dowel through the open spout of the funnel.

YOUR ATTENTION, PLEASE!

With all these marching instruments, somebody has to keep the band playing together. This is where you come in as the conductor.

This is how you conduct two beats for a two-beat march.

Cool Conducting

Your job as conductor is to keep the beat. First, stand in front of the musicians. Use your index finger or a chopstick as a conductor's baton. With your conducting hand, make these marching-beat patterns in the air.

This is the shape you make in the air when you're conducting four beats.

Sadly, Softly or Sweetly

You may want your Marching Band members to change volume — play louder or quieter. To tell the musicians how loud to play, use the hand you're not conducting with. Pat your hand downward to get them to play gently. Raise it to make them play louder.

You may also want just one instrument to play a solo. To cue the musician, point to that instrument. Use your face and arms to inspire your musicians to play sadly or sweetly — however you like. After all, you are the conductor!

Piano (soft)

Con forza (forcefully)

Molto doloroso (very sadly)

Dolce (sweetly)

One, Two, Three

Some songs, such as waltzes, have a three-beat pattern:

(1) (2) (3) (1) (2) (3)

To conduct a three-beat song, you would make this shape:

The Ants Go Marching

Get out all your instruments for this fun march. Beat your water-cooler bass drum, rattle your tambourine and buzz your tube trombone.

Em **G**

1. The ants go march-ing one by one, Hur-rah —— Hur-rah ——. The

Em **G** **B7**

ants go march-ing one by one, Hur-rah —— Hur-rah —— the

G **D7** **Em** **B7**

ants go march-ing one by one, the lit-le one stops to suck his thumb and they

Em **Am** **Em** **B7** **Em** **B7** **Em** **B7**

all go march-ing down —— to the ground —— to get

Em **B7** **Em** **B7**

out —— of the rain. Boom! Boom! Boom!

2. Two … tie his shoe
3. Three … climb a tree
4. Four … shut the door

5. Five … take a dive
6. Six … pick up sticks
7. Seven … pray to heaven

8. Eight … shut the gate
9. Nine … check the time
10. Ten … say "THE END"

Yankee Doodle

This song was so popular during the War of 1812 between the British and Americans that both sides sang it. Each side made fun of the other side with silly verses.

In marching tempo

1. Fath-er'n I went down to camp a - long with Cap - tain Good - ing.
2. Yank - ee Doo - dle went to town a - rid - ing on a pon - y - y,

There we saw the men and boys as thick as has - ty pud - ding.
Stuck a feath - er in his cap and called it mac - a - ro - ni.

Chorus

Yank - kee Doo - dle keep it up, Yan - kee Dood - le Dan - dy,

Mind the mu - sic and the step, and with the girls be hand - y.

SKIFFLE BAND

People who wanted to make music but couldn't afford to buy instruments created their own from things they had on hand — such as washboards, buckets and jugs.

For your Skiffle Band, make a tuba out of a jug, a horn out of a comb and a bass fiddle out of an old tin can. And then get ready to buzz, thunk and rattle out rhythms that will shake the roof off the house.

* Play a bucket bass
* Make a candy-box kazoo
* Twang on a tin can

SKIFFLE, JUG OR SPAZ?

Skiffle, jug and spaz are all names for a style of music that uses homemade instruments and simple rhythms. In the early 1900s, skiffle bands played African-American blues and ragtime music. During the Depression, sometimes people had "skiffle parties" to raise money to pay the rent. In New Orleans, these bands were called spaz or spasm bands. In other areas, they were called jug or jook bands because the jug was one of the main instruments. By the late 1950s, skiffle bands were playing pop songs on a guitar, washboard and tea-chest bass. Even the Beatles started out as a skiffle band.

Skiffle band music is lively and a little rough around the edges. Sometimes a musician plays a real guitar or banjo to lead the other players.

Skiffle Kazoos

Most skiffle bands feature a kazoo — an instrument that you blow or toot into to make a buzzing sound. "Blue blowing" is a skiffle band term that means to make a bluesy horn sound by blowing into a comb-and-tissue-paper kazoo. "Mirliton" is a fancy word for a kazoo.

* Comb Kazoo

Fold a piece of tissue paper in half, stick a comb inside, and you've made a kazoo. Touch your lips to the paper and sing "do, do, do" and "da, da, da." The paper will vibrate. It might even tickle. Notice how the paper vibrates more when you sing or hum louder.

* Candy-Box Kazoo

Get your hands on an empty candy box — if possible, one with a see-through window. Close the bottom flap of the box and open the top flap. Now put the open end in your mouth and hum a buzzy tune. Try a familiar song and see if any of your friends recognize your kazoo version of it.

Just a Jug

Some skiffle band players make amazing music with just a jug. Look for a large, empty and clean liquid container that has a small opening and a handle. You can use a plastic or glass jug.

✳ How You Play It

Just blowing across the top of the jug won't work — you need to buzz your lips. Tuck your bottom lip under your upper lip. Buzz a rude noise. Make your lips tight to get a high note. Keep them loose to get a low note.

Experiment by putting the mouth of the jug at different angles to your lips. The buzz you make with your lips causes the air inside the jug to move, or vibrate. The larger the jug, the louder the buzzing.

✳ Buzzing Practice

Try buzzing this pattern on your skiffle band jug:

1	2	3	4
Buzz *(high)*	**buzz** *(low)*	**buzz** *(high)*	(rest)
Buzz *(low)*	**buzz** *(medium)*	**buzz** *(high)*	(rest)

Paint-Tray Rub Board

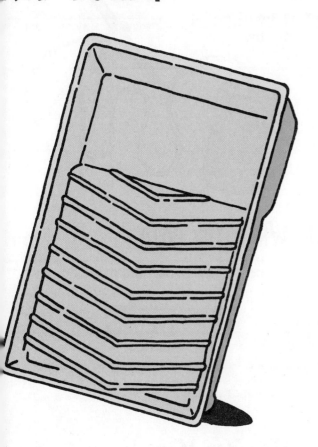

Before the washing machine was invented, people scrubbed their clothes clean on a washboard. It had a ribbed surface of glass, wood or tin, which made great rackety rhythms when rubbed with spoons. The washboard was as popular as the jug and the kazoo in many skiffle bands.

Today it's hard to find a washboard. Why not use a paint tray?

★ HOW YOU PLAY IT

Sit on a chair and put your paint-tray rub board on your lap. Lean the top against your chest. Rub, tap and scrape the spoons across the ridges. Try some Frattoire Practice on page 21. Instead of using spoons, washboard players sometimes put thimbles on their fingers to tap out a rackety rhythm.

WASHTUB BASS

The washtub was a large metal bucket used for washing clothes. Skiffle band musicians turned the washtub upside down, attached a broom handle, pulled a thick cord through the tub, and twanged the sounds of a booming bass fiddle. The washtub bass, sometimes called a gutbucket, is a string instrument.

Tin-Can Bass

No washtubs sitting around your house? You can experiment with a tin-can bass.

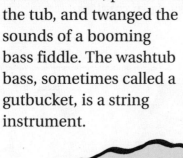

✳ WHAT YOU NEED

| large empty juice can, one end removed |
| hammer |
| nail |
| large bead |
| heavy string |
| dowel, stick or pencil |

✳ HOW YOU MAKE IT

1 Make a hole by hammering a nail into the middle of the bottom of the can.

2 Cut a length of string that reaches from your hips to the floor.

3 Tie the bead on one end of the string. Thread the other end of the string through the hole in the can. Pull through to the bead.

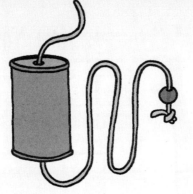

4 Tie the free end of the string around the middle of the dowel.

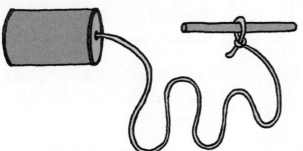

✻ How You Play It

1 Place the can on the floor. Use one foot to hold it steady.

2 Hold the dowel in one hand so that it is parallel to the floor and the string is pulled tight.

3 Use the index finger of your other hand to pluck the string. Pull the string tight and the note goes up. Loosen it and the note goes down.

Pitch Practice

Think of a baseball tossed in the air. It moves up and down. So do the notes in music. "Pitch" is the music term that indicates how high or low a note is. To practice pitches on your washtub bass, sing the skiffle band song "Old Mountain Dew" (page 61). At the end of each line, pluck the string twice, trying to match the pitch of the last note.

Bucket Bass

This bucket bass is bigger than the tin-can bass and will make louder and lower sounds because the body, or resonator, is bigger. Ask an adult to help you with this one.

✴ What You Need

saw

broom handle 1 m (39 in.) long

drill with 0.5 cm (¼ in.) bit

metal bucket or wastebasket about 40 cm (16 in.) in diameter

spike or hole punch

hammer

nylon cord 1.5 m (59 in.) long

wooden peg

✴ How You Make It

1 Saw a notch into one end of the broom handle so that it fits onto the bottom rim of the bucket.

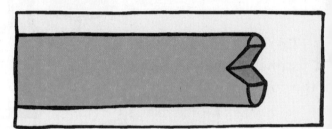

2 Drill a hole through the other end of the handle. It should be about 5 cm (2 in.) down from the top.

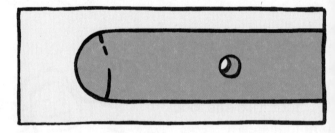

3 Punch a hole in the center of the bottom of the bucket with the spike and hammer. Thread the nylon cord through the hole. Tie the wooden peg to the end of the cord.

4 Thread the other end of the cord through the hole at the top of the broom handle. Make a secure knot.

5 Fit the notch of the broom handle onto the rim of the bucket.

* How You Play It

Place one foot on the bucket to hold it down while playing. Hold the top of the broom handle in one hand. Pluck the string with the other hand. Pull the handle back to make the string tighter. How does the pitch change? You can also hold down the string at the top of the handle. How many pitches, or notes, can you play?

* Bucket Duet

More than one person can play a bucket bass at the same time. One player plucks or slaps the string, while another person beats out a rhythm on the bucket, playing it like a drum. Try this rhythm with a friend:

	1	2	3	4
Bass:	Dhoom	dhoom	dhoom-dhoom	dhoom
Bucket drum:	rap-rap	rap-rap	(rest)	rap

The Animal Song

Here's a silly song that uses the same tune as the popular skiffle band song, "Little Brown Jug."

This song has a two-beat pattern. That means there are two beats in every bar, or section, of music. Count **1**, **2**, **1**, **2**. Each "**1**" count begins a new bar. Play a steady beat on the jug, bass and rub board. Honk the horn or ring the bell at the end of each verse.

Play on each beat.

C ①   **G** ②   **F** ①   ②

1. Al - li - ga - tor,   hedge - hog,   ant - eat - er,   bear,
2. Bull - frog, —— wood - chuck,   wol - ver - ine, —— goose,

G ①   ②   **C** ①   ②

Rat - tle - snake,   buf - fa - lo,   an - a - con - da,   hare. Honk!
Whip - poor - will,   chip - munk,   jack - al, —— moose. Honk!

3. Mud turtle, whale, glowworm, bat
   Salamander, snail and Maltese cat. Honk!

4. Polecat, dog, wild otter, rat
   Pelican, hog, dodo and bat. Honk!

5. House rat, toe rat, white bear, doe,
   Chickadee, peacock, bobolink and crow. Honk!

Old Mountain Dew

n the 1960s, people got together to sing at ootenannies. Jug bands invited the crowd to sing long with the lively chorus of songs just like this.

Verse G ... C

1. I know a place 'bout a mile down the road Where you lay down a

G

dol - lar or two; ———— If you hush up your mug they will

D7 G

slip you a jug Of that good old moun - tain dew. ————

Chorus G ... G7

They call it that good old moun - tain dew, ———————— And

C ... G

them that re - fuse it are few. ———— You may

go 'round the bend, but you'll come back a - gain For that

D7

good old moun - tain dew. ————

When its fragrance so rare starts to fill up the air
You know that you're just about through;
So you pucker your lips, and you take a few sips
Of that good old mountain dew.

3. My Aunty Jane tried a brand new perfume,
It had such a sweet smelling pu.
She was surprised when she had it analysed,
It was good old mountain dew.

SEA SHANTY BAND

Ahoy, maties! Raise the anchor and sail away. Here's a treasure chest of sailors' instruments and songs about pirates and adventures on the high seas.

* Sing your own work shanty
* Play your own pennywhistle
* Make a water-bottle fiddle

WORK SHANTIES

The crew of old sailing ships worked hard — it was haul away here and haul away there from morning to night. Pirates and sailors used to sing work songs, called shanties, to keep a rhythm that helped them heave and ho together.

For work that required one powerful lift, sailors sang a short-drag shanty, such as "Haul Away, Joe." On the last word of the chorus, they used every ounce of their strength to lift. For a slow-moving job, like raising and lowering the mainsail, they sang a long-drag shanty, such as "Blow the Man Down."

"Haul Away, Joe"

When you have chores to do, sing this version of "Haul Away, Joe." On the word "Joe," give that laundry basket or garbage bag a mighty lift. Then make up some of your own shanties.

Here's one to try on cleaning day:

Once I had to clean my room,
It nearly drove me crazy;
Way, haul away, we'll haul away, Joe.

My clothes were piled up to the roof,
My folks just say I'm lazy;
Way, haul away, we'll haul away, Joe.

Blackbeard

Edward Teach, also known as Blackbeard, tied hemp into his beard and burned it so that smoke rose up and surrounded his face. The sight was meant to terrify his victims. In the 1700s, his crew of pirates robbed trading ships off the shores of the Caribbean islands, Virginia and the Carolinas.

SHANTY BAND INSTRUMENTS

When the work was done, the crew met together in the forecastle (the crew's living quarters) to sing, dance and tell tall tales. Singers often made up their own verses while their mates played pennywhistles, concertinas and fiddles.

Woodwind Family

Pennywhistles belong to the woodwind family of instruments. These instruments are all pipes or tubes with little holes in the side or top. When you blow into a woodwind, the air inside the tube vibrates. When you cover one or more holes, you change the length of the vibrating air column and produce different notes, or pitches. The longer the column of air, the lower the note.

Reeds

f you hold a piece of grass ightly between your thumbs nd blow, the grass vibrates nd produces a squawking ound. The grass works the ame way as the reeds in some voodwind instruments, such s saxophones, clarinets, boes and bassoons — nd kazoos.

Snorkel Kazoo

No sailor worth his weight in ea salt ever played a snorkel azoo. But you can! All you eed is a snorkel, wax paper nd a rubber band.

ttach a square of wax paper o the top end of the snorkel vith the rubber band. Place he mouthpiece in your nouth. Breathe in through our nose and then hum out vith your mouth. The buzzing aper works just like a reed in regular wind instrument.

Pennywhistle

The pennywhistle is really a flute, sometimes called a tin flute. Some flutes are held horizontally, but the pennywhistle is held vertically, pointing toward the ground. Here's one that's easy to make.

* What You Need

sturdy tube, 1.5 cm (⅝ in.) in diameter and 21 cm (8¼ in.) long

pencil and ruler

large nail

mouthpiece from party horn

clear tape

* How You Make It

1 Mark and measure the six fingering holes on your tube. For the first hole, measure and mark 4.5 cm (2 in.) from the end of the tube. Measure and mark five more holes 2.5 cm (1 in.) apart.

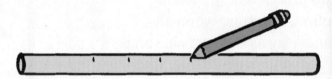

2 To make the fingering holes, punch the large nail through the top of the tube where marked.

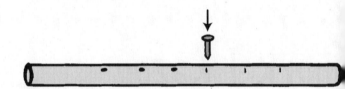

3 Place the end of the party horn mouthpiece into one end of the tube. Wrap tape around the mouthpiece and the tube.

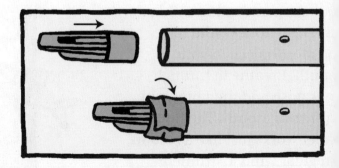

✳ How You Play It

Hold your pennywhistle so that the pads of your fingers cover the holes completely. Keep your fingers flat over the holes so they're sealed and no air leaks out. A leak will make your pennywhistle squeak.

1 Place your left thumb under the top hole. Cover the top hole with the pad of your index finger (L1). Blow gently and listen to the note.

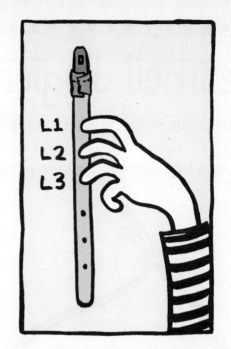

2 Cover the next hole with the middle finger (L2). Blow gently, and notice that this note sounds lower.

3 Cover the third hole with the pad of your left ring finger (L3). This note will be lower still.

4 With your left hand covering the top three notes, place your right thumb under the fourth hole. Cover the hole with the pad of your right index finger (R1).

5 Cover the fifth hole with your right middle finger (R2).

6 For the lowest note, cover the bottom hole with your right ring finger (R3).

✳ Tooting Tricks

If you flutter your fingers over the holes, you can imitate the sounds of a warbling bird. Blow very gently on the low notes. If you blow too hard, the sound will jump to a higher note.

To keep one note separate from another, here's a simple trick. Whisper "too, too, too" into the whistle. As your tongue flicks, you are separating the notes so that each sounds clear and distinct.

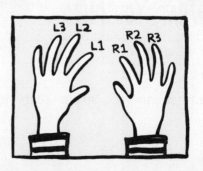

Seashell Jingler

Here's a percussion instrument that's easy to make. It's seaworthy, too. If you live inland, you can find shells at a craft or pet shop.

* How You Make It

1 Using the nail and hammer, carefully make a hole in the top of each shell. The hole needs to be big enough for the lace to pass through.

2 Tie a knot in the lace at the point where you want to start stringing the shells.

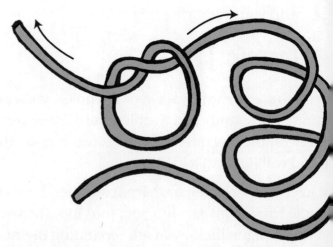

* What You Need

nail and hammer

20 seashells

thin leather shoelace, 90 cm (36 in.) long

3 String a shell. Make another knot to hold it in place. Repeat this process until all shells are on the lace. Tie the ends together.

＊ JINGLER JIGS

To play your seashell jingler, either hold it in your hand and shake it, or wear it around your neck. The shells will shake when you dance to your favorite sea shanty jig.

She Sells Seashells

When you hold a large seashell against your ear, it sounds as if the ocean is roaring inside. How come? All the sounds around you are vibrating, or resonating, inside the curved walls of the shell. As these sounds bounce back and forth on the walls of the shell, it sounds like waves lapping against the shore.

Water-Bottle Fiddle

Violins, or fiddles, were so popular by the 16th century that even the British Navy included fiddlers as part of a ship's company. Here's how to make your own version.

✳ What You Need

knife
1 L (1 qt.) plastic water bottle
40-cm (16-in.) dowel that fits into the bottle
clear tape
drill
screw eye
3 empty matchboxes
white glue
hook
steel wire or nylon string about 1 m (39 in.) long
chopstick

✳ How You Make It

1 Carefully using the knife, cut a circular hole the size of an apple on one side of the bottle about halfway down. Cut off the bottom of the bottle.

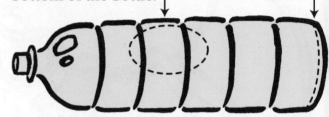

2 Put the dowel into the spout of the bottle. If it is too loose, wrap enough tape around the dowel to make it fit tightly.

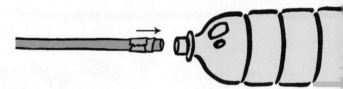

3 Ask an adult to help drill a hole in the end of the dowel. Screw the eye into the hole.

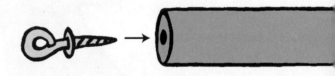

4 Glue the matchboxes together and then glue the stack of them near the bottom of the bottle.

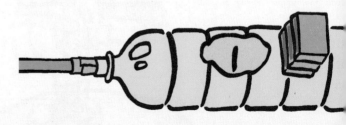

5 Attach the hook to one end of the wire. Hook the wire to the bottom rim of the bottle. Pull the wire over the matchbox bridge and wrap the other end around the screw eye so that the string is tight.

✱ How You Play It

Place the bottom of the bottle on one knee and hold the stick end in one hand. With your other hand, use the chopstick to tap the string. This note will be the lowest note you can play on your water-bottle fiddle. You can explore ways of singing above, below or with the note. If you pluck the string, you will be playing pizzicato.

What happens to the pitch if you pull back on the dowel? What if you make the string shorter by holding it down against the dowel with your fingers? In both cases, the pitch of the notes will be higher.

Folk Fiddles

There are two types of folk fiddles: the short-necked fiddle and the spike fiddle. Your water-bottle fiddle is a type of spike fiddle, because you play it vertically on your knee, not under your chin.

Blow the Man Down

Shake your seashell jingler on the "1" counts of every bar. On the words "Yeo!" and "Ho!" and each word of "Give me some time to blow the man down," pluck your water-bottle fiddle. You might want to blow a verse on your snorkel kazoo.

2. On board a Black Baller I first served my time,
   Yeo! Ho! Blow the man down!
   And in that Black Baller I wasted my prime,
   Give me some time to blow the man down.

3. With tinkers and tailors and soldiers and all,
   Yeo! Ho! Blow the man down!
   You'll seldom find sailors aboard a Black Ball,
   Give me some time to blow the man down.

4. It's larboard and starboard, you jump to the call,
   Yeo! Ho! Blow the man down!
   For Roaring Jack Williams commands the Black Ball,
   Give me some time to blow the man down.

Captain Kidd

In 1695, King William of England hired Captain Kidd to stop piracy off the coast of East Africa. Kidd chose a crew of cutthroats and robbers, who threatened mutiny unless he turned his own vessel into a pirate ship. Kidd agreed, and his murderous deeds eventually led to his capture and execution at the end of a hangman's rope.

For this lively forecastle shanty, one person sings the verse and everyone else sings the repeated refrain "As I sail." Play along on the seashell jingler, the water-bottle fiddle and the snorkel kazoo.

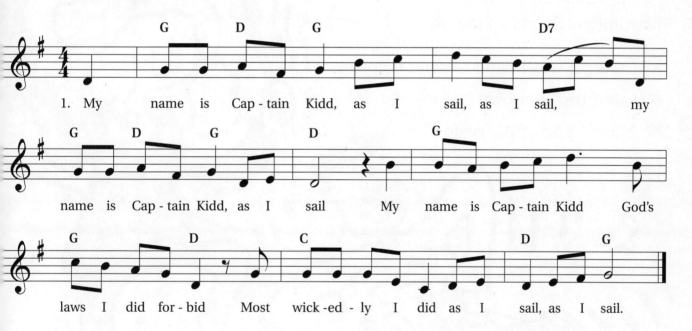

1. My name is Cap - tain Kidd, as I sail, as I sail, my name is Cap - tain Kidd, as I sail My name is Cap - tain Kidd God's laws I did for - bid Most wick -ed - ly I did as I sail, as I sail.

2. I murdered William Moore
   as I sail, as I sail
   I murdered William Moore
   as I sail
   I murdered William Moore
   And left him in his drawer
   Twenty leagues from shore
   as I sail, as I sail

3. And being crueller still
   as I sail, as I sail
   And being crueller still
   as I sail
   And being crueller still
   The gunner I did kill
   His precious blood did spill
   as I sail, as I sail

4. I was sick and nigh to death
   as I sail, as I sail
   I was sick and nigh to death
   as I sail
   I was sick and nigh to death
   I vowed with every breath
   To walk in wisdom's way
   as I sail, as I sail

TRASH BAND

Raid the recycling bin and check out neighborhood garage sales. You and your friends can turn pop cans, clay flower pots, air vents, door stoppers and hub caps into fantastic instruments that keep the beat.

* Create a Trash Band Sound Sculpture
* Compose your own music
* Make a pop bottle scale

♪ Music Notes

Rhythm Sense

Rhythm, or the pattern of beats, can be fast or slow. This is called the tempo of the music. The beats can be hard or soft, depending on the volume of the music. And they can be harsh or smooth, sharp or muffled — this gives the notes their special tone. These are all elements of music you can play around with to create different effects.

Pop-Can Stompers

Why not start your Trash Band with your own trash? Take two empty pop cans and scrunch them with your feet so they stay attached to your shoes when you walk. This is definitely an outdoor activity! Clang, clatter and chonk your way down the street. Get a group of friends together, put on your pop-can stompers and work out some neat feet beats.

Try stomping the beat of this old sidewalk chant. Clatter or chonk a bit harder on the bold beats.

1	2
Step on a	**crack,**
Break my	**back.**
Step on a	**line,**
Break my	**spine.**

TRASH RHYTHMS

Don't forget that metal trash can! Experiment with tapping the bottom, inside, outside, rim and handle with your hands or with a wooden spoon. Get in touch with your "rhythm bone" and tap out the **bold** beats of a song that's familiar and easy, such as "Twinkle, Twinkle, Little Star."

1	2	1	2
Twin-kle,	**twin**-kle,	**lit**-tle	**star,**
How I	**won**-der	**what** you	**are.**
Up a-	**bove** the	**world** so	**high,**
Like a	**dia**-mond	**in** the	**sky,**
Twin-kle,	**twin**-kle,	**lit**-tle	**star,**
How I	**won**-der	**what** you	**are.**

Trash Can Fun

✳ Beat the rhythm on your trash can first slowly, then fast. Which tempo sounds better? Try the same thing with your pop-can stompers.

✳ Use a wooden spoon to beat out the rhythm on the top of your trash can. First tap lightly, then really pound it. Which volume sounds better? What happens when you beat the rhythm on the sides of the trash can? How does that change the volume?

✳ Use the wooden spoon on a pop can and clang out the beats. How is the tone different from the sound of the spoon on your trash can?

Pop-Bottle Notes

Raid the recycling bin for the perfect set of glass pop bottles. Or try bottled water bottles!

* What You Need

five 750-mL (26-oz.) glass bottles all the same size

funnel

pitcher of water

* How You Make It

1 Line up the bottles on a table. Use a funnel to pour water into the bottles. Each bottle needs a different amount of water to make a different note.

2 Starting with the bottle on the left, add a few centimeters (inches) of water. Add a little more water to each of the other bottles. The bottle on the right should have the most water.

3 Try tuning your pop-bottle notes using piano keys or a pitch pipe.

* How You Play It

Blow across the top of each bottle to produce a note. Blowing causes the air inside the bottle to vibrate, or shake. If there is a lot of water and less air in the bottle, the air vibrates quickly and produces a higher note. If there is less water and more air, the note is lower, because the air vibrates more slowly.

* A Striking Observation

You can turn your water-filled bottles into percussion instruments by striking them with a wooden spoon. But something strange happens. The bottle that sounded low when you blew across the top now sounds high when you strike it. That's because when you tap a bottle, the water vibrates, not the air. The more water, the lower the note. The less water, the higher the note. Check this out by blowing into one of your bottles and then striking it.

* Rub It In

When you rub glass, you get a completely different kind of sound. For the best results, use a crystal glass. Start rubbing the rim slowly with a damp finger. A low note will ring from the glass. As you continue to rub the rim, the vibrations get stronger. This sets off a series of other notes that sound together. They are called harmonics.

Stay Tuned

The only way to play in tune with other musicians is to tune your instruments together. A tuning fork comes in handy for this. When you strike the fork, it vibrates. To hear the vibrations, hold the fork close to your ear or place it on a wooden surface. The vibrations will cause the surface to resonate, and the sound will be louder. A tuning fork vibrates at 440 vibrations per second. This produces the note A, which is called concert pitch. All over the world, instruments are tuned to this pitch.

♪ MUSIC NOTES

Bell Maestro

Imagine growing up to be a carillonneur or bell master! You would have studied campanology — the art of carillon ringing. A carillon is a group of at least 23 bells hung in a fixed position in a tower — like Canada's Peace Tower on Parliament Hill in Ottawa. The bells sound different notes from high to low so they can play any melody. The keyboard of a carillon is called a clavier. When the bell master presses down on a key, the clapper strikes the inside of the bell and plays the note.

BELL BEATS

School bells, church bells, cow bells, jingle bells. Did you know that all bells are percussion instruments? A bell makes music when it is struck with a clapper or hammer. The clapper is either held in the hand or fastened to the inside of the bell.

Clay-Pot Bells

Collect some clay flower pots and turn them into your own miniature carillon. Make sure the pots don't have any cracks in them. Cracked pots will not produce a ringing sound.

✳ WHAT YOU NEED

clay pots of various sizes

large wooden beads

heavy string

frame for holding bells

wooden spoon

✳ HOW YOU MAKE THEM

1 For each pot, select a bead that is larger than the drainage hole. Thread the string through the bead and knot it so that the bead won't slip off. Thread the string through the drainage hole and tie the loose end to the frame.

2 Tie the bells to the frame according to size — largest to smallest. The largest bell will have the lowest pitch, and the smallest will have the highest.

✳ HOW YOU PLAY THEM

Play the bells by gently striking them on the outside or inside with a wooden spoon. Experiment with single taps and repeated taps. Play two bells at once.

Instead of tying the bells left to right, try hanging them, one bell above another. Run the wooden spoon down the tower of bells.

GOING, GOING, GONG!

Gongs are flying saucer-shaped bells. Like bells, gongs vibrate when struck. The big difference is that gongs ring near the center and bells ring near the rim.

Hub caps make great gongs for a Trash Band. You can strike them, tap them or just bang away. If you've got a pair of hub caps, try turning them into cymbals.

Get a Gong

Hang up almost any flat piece of metal and you've got a gong. Try some old frying pans. What different gong sounds do you get from an aluminum frying pan and a cast iron one? Does the size of the pan make any difference? Use a chopstick to gong your gong, and then switch to something else. Does the sound change?

GONG! GONG!

GONG GONG!

Door-Stopper Sprong

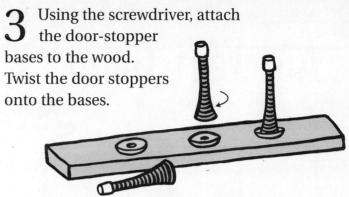

Attach some door stoppers to a piece of wood and sprong out a beat.

✴ What You Need

Length of wood 30 cm x 4 cm x 1.5 cm (12 in. x ½ in. x ½ in.)

Drill with a bit slightly smaller than the door-stopper screw

Screwdriver

3 spring-type door stoppers

✴ How You Make It

1 Place the board on a work table. Mark three spots equal distances apart on the top of the board.

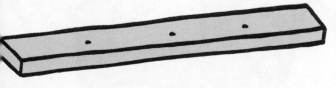

2 Drill a hole at each mark. (You may want adult help with this step.)

3 Using the screwdriver, attach the door-stopper bases to the wood. Twist the door stoppers onto the bases.

✴ How You Play It

Pluck the stoppers one at a time and let them wiggle and vibrate. Put the sprong base on a table and the vibrations will sound louder, because the table surface vibrates, too. Experiment by placing the sprong base on different surfaces, such as a filing cabinet and a wood floor. Each surface will resonate (vibrate) differently.

Air-Vent Guiro

Cymbals

When two or more similar objects are crashed together to make music, they are called "concussion" instruments. Old cooking-pot lids make perfect cymbals. Or for a really big bang, try two metal garbage can lids. What happens if you tie them onto your feet and then crash them together? (Some feat!)

If anyone in the neighborhood is renovating a house, find out if they're pitching out any old forced-air vents. You can turn them into guiros. Guiros come from Latin America. Traditionally made from gourds, they have notched surfaces, and are played by scraping a stick across the notches or bumps. For your air-vent guiro, cover any rough edges with tape so you don't get scraped when you scrape it!

Trash Band Sound Sculpture

Now that you have collected and constructed all this musical junk, build yourself a sound sculpture as your ultimate Trash Band instrument. You'll need a frame to hang instruments on — the legs of an upside-down chair are ideal. Hang your gongs, chimes and bells so that it's easy for you to play them. Lay things like the door-stopper sprong and the air-vent guiro on the floor where you can grab them easily. It's time to improvise and compose your own musical score.

Stomp

Stomp is the name of a popular performance troupe from Britain that uses junk, household items and industrial objects for musical instruments. Everything Stomp does is based on rhythm. In one composition, or piece of music, the players use brooms and dustpans. In another, they make music by walking on enormous oil drums.

COMPOSE YOUR OWN MUSIC

The composer puts together the elements of music — such as beat, rhythm and tempo — to create a song or musical piece called a composition. The actual pattern of notes that is written down on paper is called a musical score. Many composers start creating a new piece of music by just improvising.

Improvise

Making up your own rhythm patterns and musical sounds on the spot is called improvising. To improvise, first you need to know the sound of each of the instruments you've made. Which one makes a shimmering sound, a crashing sound, a tinkling sound? What other sounds can you make when you play them?

You may want to include instruments from other bands in this book. Start with a woodwind, such as the pennywhistle from the Sea Shanty Band, and a string instrument, such as the bucket bass from the Skiffle Band. Now organize the instruments so that you can play them easily.

Get Inspired!

Inspiration can come from almost anything — an idea, feeling, story, theme or what you had last night for supper. Pick the first idea that comes into your head and give it a beat, rhythm and tempo with one of your Trash Band instruments.

Improvising with friends leads to many musical discoveries. If one band member starts an improvised rhythm, you can echo back the same sounds or respond by playing them backward. You can play with rhythmic patterns and tone effects. The magical thing about improvisation is that you never play your musical score the same way twice!

A Haunting Score

Let your imagination take you on a musical tour of a haunted house. You may want to try this musical score to start with and then head off in your own direction. Record your performance and play it back.

Here are the instruments your band will need for this score: a comb (rub your thumb along its teeth to make a cricket sound), hub cap gong, air-vent guiro, frying pan gong, clay-pot bells, garbage can cymbals, and claves — two hardwood sticks that you strike together (see page 134). If you don't have all of these instruments, find other things you can use to make percussion sounds.

• Silence for few moments

• Comb crickets

• Shimmer of a hub cap gong
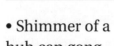

• Grating of air-vent guiro — start quietly, then build to a louder sound (crescendo), then gradually go back to quiet (decrescendo)

• Steady beat on a frying pan gong while playing clay-pot bells to an unsteady beat
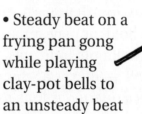

• Silence

• Crash of garbage can cymbals

• Ten seconds of crashes

• Silence
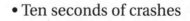

• Claves struck once

WHAT'S THE SCORE?

You have an inspiration for a Trash Band song, and you want to write it down so that your friends can play it along with you. When you've written down a musical idea, you've created a musical score. It includes all the parts that you want the members of your band to play and sing.

Composers use lots of music symbols to write their scores. They use whole notes, half notes, quarter notes, sixteenth notes, thirty-second notes — even sixty-fourth notes — to represent beats that you hold, or play, for a certain length of time. A half note indicates that the beat is played half as long as a whole note; a quarter note lasts a quarter as long as a whole note; an eighth note lasts an eighth as long as a whole note, and so on. Composers also use whole rests, half rests, quarter rests and so on to indicate that the musicians take a break — they don't play on the rests. Composers write their notes and rests on a music staff. It has five parallel lines, and the lines indicate the pitch of the notes. If you look at a song that's been written down, or notated, you'll see notes moving up and down the staff.

For your Trash Band score, you can do the same thing using dots, lines, shapes, colors and images.

* Dots

For a steady rhythm, draw a series of dots.

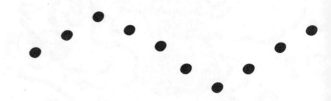

For a melody, make the dots go up the page for higher notes and down the page for lower notes.

For louder notes, make larger dots. For quieter notes, make smaller dots.

For an unsteady rhythm, use a cluster of dots.

* Lines

Draw a straight line for an even tone.

Draw a wavy line for a smooth note that changes back and forth in pitch, from high to low.

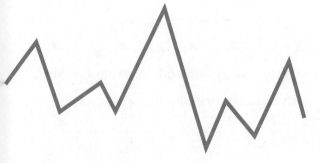

Draw a jagged line for rapid jumps of sound from high to low.

* Shapes

Use geometric shapes such as squares, triangles or rectangles to indicate rests.

Draw a spiral, a loop or a figure eight. How do these sound when you play them?

* Color

Use color to show the tone of your score. Will bright blue indicate a loud, bright sound? Will light blue be a soft, mellow sound?

* Images

You can cut out pictures from magazines and place them on graph paper. A bright object, like a sun up high on the paper, could be played as a loud, bright sound. How about using the board game Snakes and Ladders? You can have your musicians slide (or glissando) their notes down a snake and sing a scale while going up the rungs of a ladder. Or try a road map. Color-code roads, cities, rivers and railway lines. Each line represents a different instrument. If the road goes up, play higher. If you come to a city, have a pause. You can make up your own rules for your score. Why not try them forward, backward and upside down?

My Mama Don't Allow

Pull out all your Trash Band instruments and play along to this song. When a verse says that a certain instrument is not allowed, you get to have fun by ignoring the singer and playing a solo verse on the forbidden instrument. Do as many verses as you like. With a group of friends, you can all play together when you sing "My Mama don't allow no Trash Band 'round here."

1. My Mom - ma don't al - low (My Mom - ma don't al - low) no sing - ing 'round here. My Mom - ma don't al - low (My Mom - ma don't al -low) no sing - ing 'round here. I don't care —— what my Mom - ma don't al - low, I'll sing an - y - how.

2. My Momma don't allow no can stomping ...

3. My Momma don't allow no bell ringing ...

4. My Momma don't allow no cymbal crashing ...

5. My Momma don't allow no trash band ...

Pick It Up

Use a different Trash Band instrument to keep the beat for each verse. Play the instrument on the words that are in bold. On the chorus, have all the instruments join in with a steady beat.

Deborah Dunleavy

Chorus

Pick it up and put it in a gar - bage can

Pick it up and give it to a gar - bage man

Pick it up and put it in a gar - bage can

Pick it up and make it a clean - er land

1. We'd **like** to mention
There's a **lot** of tension
About the **gar**-bage on our **street.**
It's **our** intention
To **pay** attention
To the **mess** around our **feet.**
We make **no** pretention
That an **ounce** of prevention
Could **cure** the problem right **now.**
We're the **clean**-up convention
Of **this** dimension
And **we** can show you **how.**
Chorus

2. We **should** explain
It **hurts** the terrain
It **chokes** up the air we **breathe.**
It's **too** insane
It's **in**-humane
This **trash** and junk we **leave.**
We **must** restrain
We **must** refrain
From **us**-ing and abusing this **place.**
Let's **all** maintain
A **clean** campaign
Say "**No!** No more to this **waste.**"
Chorus

3. We **make** correct
Our **self** respect
By **car**-ing for the planet **Earth.**
No **more** neglect
We **must** protect
Our **lives** and what they're **worth.**
We **do** reflect
We **do** connect
On the **chan**-ges we can **make.**
We **on**-ly get
What **we** expect
That's **true** make no mis-**take!**
Chorus

A CAPPELLA JAM BAND

Bop-bop
be-bop
bop-bop
be-bop

Here's a band just for voices. Singing without musical instruments is called singing a cappella. Lots of people sing a cappella in the bathtub. Sometimes people sing a cappella when they work, either to pass the time or to keep a rhythm that helps get the job done. You and your friends can use just your singing voices to make wonderful music — from rap to scat to be-bop and doo-wop.

* Learn how to harmonize
* Create a Scat Orchestra
* Jam with a Voice Box Band

YOUR AMAZING VOICE

Your voice is an amazing instrument that can whisper, shout, talk and sing. When it's singing, it can sing high and low, loud and quiet, fast and slow. It can warble and trill, belt out a tuneful tune, hum a lullaby and imitate all sorts of band instruments. To make any of these sounds, it takes your lungs, throat, mouth, nose and chest all working together.

Bump in Your Throat

Gently rub your hand up and down the front of your throat. The bump you feel is your Adam's apple. It is the front part of your larynx, also know as your voice box. It is made of cartilage, the same substance that you can feel at the tip of your nose.

Folded across your larynx are two bands of elastic-like tissue called vocal chords. When you talk or sing, your larynx works like a muscle, pulling the vocal chords together. This makes the space between the muscles smaller, and the air passing by makes the chords vibrate.

Inside Your Voice Box

Blow up a balloon and pinch the stem tight with your thumb and finger so no air escapes. Stretch the stem and let some of the air out of the balloon. Listen to the sound it makes. Pull tighter and the note will get higher.

Your larynx works in the same way. When the muscles in your larynx are pulled tighter, the sound gets higher. Place your hand against the front of your throat. Sing a low note. Now sing a high note. Feel how the muscles make your larynx jump up as you switch your voice from low to high.

Great Vibes!

In The Magic Flute, *an opera by Mozart, the soprano who plays the Queen of the Night is expected to sing the highest note ever written for a vocalist. It is called high F. The singer's vocal chords need to move at 1400 vibrations per second to hit that note dead on.*

Vocal Range

Have you ever wondered why some people have really high voices and others have really low voices? People with high voices have short, thin vocal chords. People with lower voices have longer, thicker vocal chords. Longer vocal chords vibrate more slowly, making the notes lower.

YOUR OWN RESONATORS

A violin or guitar needs a hollow body to amplify the sound, or make the strings sound louder. Vocal chords also need resonators to amplify voice sounds. Your chest is one of your own resonators. Your throat is another. Place your hands on either side of your throat and sing up and down. Feel the sound resonating in your throat.

Jungle Call

Fill your lungs with air. Hold your hand on your chest. Sing the deepest, lowest note you can. You should feel your chest vibrating. This time make a jungle call by singing "ah-ah-ah" (low-high-low) while beating on your chest. (Move over, Tarzan.)

Pinch Your Nose

Believe it or not, even your nose acts like a resonator. Sing "me-me-me-me-me" while pinching your nose. Feel your nose vibrating?

Say AH!

The way you shape your mouth changes the sounds you make. Say the vowels A, E, I, O and U. Notice how you change your mouth shape. The shape of your mouth also changes the pitch of a sound, or how high or low it is.

Try this:

Open your mouth wide as if you are going to say "ah."

Cup your hands slightly and clap them together in front of your mouth.

Change the shape of your mouth to "ee." Clap again.

Notice how the pitch of the "ah" clap is lower than the pitch of the "ee" clap.

Choir Voices

The highest voice in a choir is called the soprano. The next highest is the alto. Lower yet is the tenor, followed by the baritone. The lowest voice of all is the bass.

SINGING TOGETHER

When you sing the same notes at the same time with another singer, you are singing in unison. If you and a friend sing different notes at the same time and the sound is pleasing, call it harmony. If your voices clash or sound weird, then your pet might run for cover. These unpleasant sounds are called dissonance — or just plain noise.

Barbershop Quartet

Singers in a barbershop quartet make harmonies by singing a chord for each word in the song. A chord is a group of notes that sound pleasing when played or sung together. The four voices in a barbershop quartet are lead, tenor, baritone and bass.

You don't have to get a haircut to sing harmonies. With four people you can make up your own barbershop quartet harmonies.

Try this:

• The first person takes the lead part and sings the word "oh."

• The second person takes the bass part and sings "oh" a note lower.

• The third person takes the baritone part and tries to sing "oh" between the lead and the bass.

• The fourth person takes the tenor part and tops it off by singing "oh" a note higher than the lead singer.

• Now do the same thing with the word "my." Move on to "darling." Have you caught on to the song? Try this opening line in four-part harmony:

Oh, my darling, oh, my darling,

Oh, my darling Clementine.

☀ Did You Ever See ...?

Test your harmonies — "down by the bay." In this familiar song, one person sings a line and another echoes it back in harmony. Both singers sing the last two lines together. Repeat the song and make up your own question each time.

Down by the bay, *(echo)*

Where the watermelons grow, *(echo)*

Back to my home, *(echo)*

I dare not go. *(echo)*

For if I do, *(echo)*

My mother would say: *(echo)*

"Did you ever see a pig wearing a wig, *(together)*

Down by the bay?" *(together)*

Chords

Chords are notes that are sung or played together to create harmony. Doh, mi, soh is a major chord that makes a pleasant sound when sung. To make the harmony sound sad, you could sing re, fa, la. It is a minor chord. The piano, guitar, harp and vibraphone are just a few of the instruments that you can play chords on.

 **SOUND BITES**

All That Jazz!

Jazz music started about a hundred years ago with the rhythms and harmonies of African-American folk music, such as lullabies, spirituals and "field hollers" (work songs). Musicians began mixing these styles of music with European hymns, marches, waltzes and light-opera tunes.

Early jazz bands played for picnics, weddings, parades and funerals. They used a trumpet for the lead melody, a clarinet for playing around the lead, a trombone for slides, a tuba for a bass sound and drums for rhythm. Jazz music includes lots of different styles — from blues and bebop to swing, Dixieland and ragtime.

SCAT SINGING

Jazz singers make up "scat" words to fit in with the rhythm and melody of a song. Scat words are not really words — they're syllables and sounds, like "doo bee doo bee doo."

Many scat singers make their voices sound like musical instruments. Try scatting these jazzy words. What instruments do they make you think of?

Doo bee doo bee doo

Tweet tweet tweet

Scoo bee doo bop bop

Ding dang ding dang ding-dang ding

Wha wha duh duh

Scat Orchestra

You can make up your own Scat Orchestra with scat words that you sing high and low, fast and slow. Count four beats to lead in. Then snap your fingers to the beat and make the scat words fit in and around those beats.

Here's one to try with four singers. Each person chooses a line. When everyone is scatting together, this should sound like a cool jazz band.

	1	2	1	2
Singer 1	**Zing**	zing	(rest)	zing-zing
Singer 2	**Doo**	ba	doo	ba
Singer 3	**Bop-bop**	be-bop	bop-bop	be-bop
Singer 4	**WOW** ———————————			

VOICE BOX BAND

Get together with friends and make your voices sound like musical instruments in a band.

Muted Trumpet

1 Keep lips closed but loose. Upper and lower teeth should almost touch.

2 Sing "taa-taa too-too" sounds so that the lips vibrate.

3 Pinch nostrils with thumb and index finger of one hand and cup the hand over your mouth.

4 Cup the other hand over the first hand and move the fingers back and forth to create the wavy vibrato sound.

Electric Guitar

1 Smile.

2 In a high voice, sing "dear-dear-dear-dear" so quickly that the "ea" part is barely heard. Keep smiling and only move your bottom lip.

3 Put an accent or emphasis on the "d" to create the electric sound of the strings as they are plucked one at a time.

Jazzy Bass

1 Pout.

2 Sing "dhoom, dhoom, dhoom" in a low, soft voice so that your bottom lip makes a little popping sound with each note.

Cool Brushes

1 Keep your teeth together and lips apart.

2 Whisper the sounds "chsh-chsh-chu-chsh" over and over again.

Jam It Up!

Now your A Cappella Band is ready to jam. Try "A Tisket, A Tasket," a folk tune made famous by one of the world's best jazz singers, Ella Fitzgerald. Start with the swish of the brushes, add the boom of the bass, and top it off with the muted toot of the trumpet.

A tisket, a tasket,
A red and yellow basket,
I wrote a letter to my love,
And on the way I dropped it.

DOO-WOP, DOO-WOP

In New York City in the 1950s, teenagers would gather on street corners to sing the pop songs of the day. They couldn't afford musical instruments so they used their voices to imitate the sounds of bass guitars and snare drums. Some groups made up their own songs and recorded them. Out of that era came famous doo-wop groups such as the Platters, the Four Seasons and the Persuasions.

More Scat

Like jazz singers, doo-wop singers use scat words in their songs. In a doo-wop group, there is usually one lead singer whose voice is high, either soprano or tenor. The lead sings the melody of the song. The backup singers harmonize or make rhythmic scat sounds with their voices — just as in a barbershop quartet.

Crooning Doo-Wop

Crooning is a sweet, smooth way of singing that is used in doo-wop songs with a slow tempo. Take a scat phrase such as "oo-whaa" or "woo-ooo" and croon some harmonies with your friends. Remember, a harmony is a sound that is pleasing to the ear. You will know it when you hear it.

Doo-Wop Backup

It's time to put a doo-wop group together and start scatting. With doo-wop songs, the singers keep a steady beat by tapping their toes or snapping their fingers. Give this a try and you'll have all the backup sounds of a doo-wop group.

‖ This is a repeat sign. In steps 2, 3 and 4, repeat the scat sounds between the signs.

1 Everyone taps toes or snaps fingers to a steady beat. (Count 1 , 2 , 3 , 4 , 1 , 2 , 3 , 4 .)

2 The person with the lowest voice sings the bass part:

1	2	3	4	1	2	3	4
‖: Bomp	bomp	bomp	bomp-dee	bomp	bomp	bomp,	(rest)
Bomp-dee	bomp	bomp	bomp,	bomp-dee	bomp	bomp	bomp. :‖

3 The next voice sings:

1	2	3	4	1	2	3	4
‖: Ooo ——————		wah, ——————		ooo ——————		wah, ——————	
Ooo ——————		wah, ——————		ooo ——————		wah, ——————	:‖

4 In a high nasal voice, the next person sings:

1	2	3	4
‖: Dip-de	dip-de	dip.	(rest)	Dip-de	dip-de	dip.	(rest)
Dip-de	dip-de	dip	dip,	Dip-de	dip-de	dip,	dip· :‖

MAKE IT A RAP

In New York City in the mid-1970s, young African-Americans began chanting rhymes about the hard conditions of life in their neighborhoods. They called their music "rap." "Rap" is short for "rapport," which means a special understanding or harmony between people. You probably have great rapport with your friends in your Voice Box Band. How about with your teacher?

Rap Rhythm

Rap music lyrics are spoken, not sung, and the rhythm is full of surprises. Often the stress or accent falls between the beats. These in-between beats are called "off-beats." This kind of rhythm is called syncopation. Here's how it works:
1 **and** 2 **and** 3 **and** 4 **and**.

Try your own syncopated rhythm by clapping on the off-beats — on each **and**:

Count	1	**and**	2	**and**	3	**and**	4	**and**
	On	**off**	on	**off**	on	**off**	on	**off**
Clap		*clap*		*clap*		*clap*		*clap*

Rap Away!

Practice rapping the chorus for "TV-itis" (page 111). For this rap-like chant, count in the beats before starting: **1, 2, 3, 4**. Add some Voice Box Band sounds. One singer makes a cool brushes sound, another makes a jazzy bass sound.

1	and	2	and	3	and	4	and	1	and	2	and	3	and	4	and
T -	V -	it -	is,					I've	got	it	bad.				
	clap		*clap*		*clap*		*clap*		*clap*		*clap*		*clap*		*clap*
T -	V -	it -	is,					It	drives	me	mad.				
	clap		*clap*		*clap*		*clap*		*clap*		*clap*		*clap*		*clap*

Skit Skat

This upbeat song has all sorts of scat words.
Use them or make up your own.

© Deborah Dunleavy

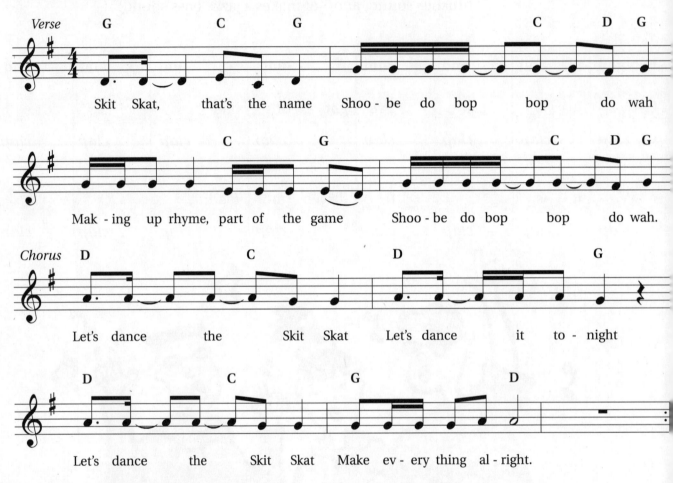

Verse

Skit Skat, that's the name Shoo - be do bop bop do wah

Mak - ing up rhyme, part of the game Shoo - be do bop bop do wah.

Chorus

Let's dance the Skit Skat Let's dance it to - night

Let's dance the Skit Skat Make ev - ery thing al - right.

2. Take silly word, fit it to the beat,
    Shoobe do bop bop do wah.
    We'll be scoobe do bop bopping down to our feet,
    Shoobe do bop bop do wah.
    Chorus

3. Take off hat, give head a shake,
    Rama rama ding dong ping pong.
    Shoulders to fingers, quiver and quake,
    Rama rama ding dong ping pong.
    Chorus

4. Twist hips like lemon peel,
    Rama rama ding dong ping pong.
    Show everybody how good it feel,
    Rama rama ding dong ping pong.
    Chorus

5. Pretzel legs, give them a twirl,
    Shoe hop hop run bop.
    Kick them up boy, kick them up girl,
    Shoe hop hop run bop.
    Chorus

TV-itis

© Deborah Dunleavy

Your Voice Box Band practiced the chorus of this song on page 109. Now try the whole rap.

Love to watch the TV screen,
Noon and night and in between.
My breakfast, lunch, midnight snack —
I get a case of TV attack.

Chorus:
TV-itis (*clap, clap*)
I've got it bad
TV-itis (*clap, clap*)
It drives me mad.

Flip the channel, turn the dial —
Video hits, video style.
My parents say I'll lose my sight
If I watch it late at night.

Chorus

Early morning cartoon show,
Sports events — Go team Go!
Games and prizes, interviews,
Soaps and series, evening news.

Chorus

COOL BODY JIVE

Your arms swing. Your feet tap. Your knees knock. Your fingers snap. Your whole body is a rapping, tapping musical instrument. Make up music with your head, your hands and your feet — and use your whole body to keep the beat!

* Bibble your lips and pop your cheeks
* Learn African hand-jive rhythms
* Try some fancy foot drumming

MEOW

JUMP

JIVE ALIVE

From the top of your head to the tips of your toes you can make terrific music. Stand in front of a mirror and discover all the ways you can make rhythmic sounds with your body.

Head: *knock, pop, sing, hum, sniff, yodel, sigh*

Fingers: *snap, click, flick*

Hands: *clap, rub, slap, wipe, slide*

Stomach: *toom*

Knees: *knock*

Thighs: *thump*

Feet: *jump, shuffle, slide, bounce, stomp*

Toes: *tip-tap, tip-tap*

Stomping and Popping

Combine foot stomping with finger snapping, or knee knocking with head popping. How many different ways can you make up a cool body jive? Try some rhythms with this four-beat jive combo:

1	2	3	4	1	2	3	4	1	2	3	4
snap	snap	toom	toom	jump			clap-clap	clap	knock	knock	
Fingers		*Stomach*		*Feet*			*Hands*		*Knees*		

Body-Jive Chant

A chant is a group of words that are spoken together in a musical way. You've probably heard chants at football games and in the playground. Try this one.

Chickee-Paw Chant

Say, "Chickee-paw, chickee-paw, chickee-paw-paw-paw." Notice the beat that the words make. Say it again and clap on the word "paw."

1	2	3	4
Chickee- **paw,** chickee-**paw,**	chickee-**paw-paw-**	**paw**	
Clap	clap	clap	clap

One person leads the chant with voice and actions. Others follow by echoing the leader's chant and actions each time.

Leader: *(Clap hands)*
Chickee-**paw**, chickee-**paw**, chickee-**paw-paw-paw**.

Followers: *(Echo line and clap)*

Leader: *(Tap knees)*
Chickee-**paw**, chickee-**paw**, chickee-**paw-paw-paw**.

Followers: *(Echo line and tap knees)*

Leader: *(Snap fingers)*
Chickee-**paw**, chickee-**paw**, chickee-**paw-paw-paw**.

Followers: *(Echo line and snap fingers)*

LET'S FACE IT

You and your face can make incredible music. You can "bibble" your lips, pop your cheeks and drum your face. Pick an easy song and bibble, pop and drum away. It might take a bit of practice!

Teach face music to your friends and get together for a jam session. Record yourselves, and be sure that someone is taking pictures!

Lip Bibbling

Make a motorboat sound with your lips and hum at the same time — now you're lip bibbling.

Try a familiar song, such as "You Are My Sunshine," and bibble away.

* Bibble Practice

You are my sunshine, my only sunshine,

You make me happy, when skies are gray.

You'll never know, dear, how much I love you

Please don't take my sunshine away.

Cheek Popping

Puff out your cheeks with air and keep your lips tightly puckered. Tap your cheeks with your hands so that the air pops out in a rhythm.

Here's another way to make a popping sound. Put your index finger into your mouth. When you pull your finger out, let it pop against the inside of your cheek.

Cheek Drumming

Yawn so you have a hollow space inside your mouth. Make a great big "OH" shape with your lips. Tap out a rhythm on your cheeks. To make the notes higher or lower, change the shape of the hollow inside your mouth by moving your tongue around.

Face Band Song

Get your friends together to bibble, pop and drum. Have each person play one part.

Bibble:	**The bear went over the mountain,**
Cheek pop:	**The bear went over the mountain,**
Cheek drum:	**The bear went over the mountain,**
Bibble:	**To see what he could see. POP!**

HAND-JIVE BEATS

You'll find kids doing hand jives with clapping patterns in playgrounds and schoolyards all over the world. Some are difficult and take a lot of practice. Grab a friend and take it one clap at a time with these patterns.

Two-Beat Hand Jive

Beat 1: Clap your hands together.

Beat 2: Put palms facing out and clap your partner's palms. Start slowly and increase the tempo (speed) when you feel comfortable.

Four-Beat Hand Jive

Beat 1: Clap your hands together.

Beat 2: Clap your partner's right hand with your right hand.

Beat 3: Clap your hands together.

Beat 4: Clap your partner's left hand with your left hand.

Eight-Beat Hand Jive

Once you have mastered the four-beat pattern, add four more beats.

Beat 5:
Clap your hands together.

Beat 6:
Put palms facing out and clap your partner's palms.

Beat 7:
Cross your arms and tap your left shoulder with your right hand and your right shoulder with your left hand.

Beat 8:
Clap your hands on your knees.

Hand Claps

Your hands can make many sounds. When you clap them flat, they will sound different …

than when you clap them cupped.

If you brush them together, the sound will be different again.

AFRICAN HAND CLAPPING

Hand clapping is a very old and important part of African music. Babies begin learning traditional clapping rhythms while sitting on the laps of their elders, and at a very young age, children follow rhythm patterns of whole hand-clapping songs. The Shona people of Ghana and Zimbabwe call the art of hand clapping "makwa."

Shona Hand-Clapping Song

Many African clapping songs follow a four-beat pattern. Here's an African clapping pattern to try.

A = sweep your hands **Away** in an upward circular motion

T = clap your hands **Together**

L = clap your partner's **Left** palm with your left palm

B = hit the **Back** of your hands against the back of your partner's hands

R = clap your partner's **Right** palm with your right palm

Try these combinations:

✳ A T, A T, B T, B T

✳ R L T, R L T, B T, B T, R L T

FOOT DRUMMING

Dancers use foot sounds and patterns all the time. Flamenco, tap, clogging and soft shoe are just some of the ways that dancers keep the beat with their feet.

You can make music with just your feet. That's what tap dancers do. In Australia, the techno-wizards of tap are known as the Tap Dogs. They give foot drumming performances all over the world.

Put on some hard-soled shoes and try these four-beat patterns. Go ahead — make up your own fancy footwork and teach it to your friends.

Foot Drumming Score 1: "Sneak Up"

	1	2	3	4
(L foot)	Tip - toe	tip - toe	tip - toe	heel
(R foot)	Tip-toe	tip-toe	tip-toe	heel
(Both feet)	Jump			

Foot Drumming Score 2: "Slip Sliding Away"

	1	2	3	4
(L foot)	Thump-thump-	thump	(rest)	(rest)
(R foot)	Thump-thump-	thump	(rest)	(rest)
(L foot to left)	Slide ————————————————		(rest)	(rest)
(L foot to center)	Slide ————————————————		(rest)	(rest)
(R foot to right)	Slide ————————————————		(rest)	(rest)
(R foot to center)	Slide ————————————————		(rest)	(rest)

"Miss Mary Mack"

The eight-beat clapping pattern fits with this hand-jive song. After you've tried these verses, make up your own. Here's a start:

Miss Mary Mink, Mink, Mink,
All dressed in pink, pink, pink

Miss Mar-y Mack, Mack, Mack, All dressed in
black, black, black, With sil-ver but-tons, but-tons,
but-tons, Up and down her back, back, back.

She went to the river, river, river,
Couldn't get across, 'cross, 'cross,
She spent five dollars, dollars, dollars,
On an old gray horse, horse, horse.

The horse wouldn't pull, pull, pull,
So she swapped it for a bull, bull, bull,
And the bull wouldn't holler, holler, holler,
Swapped it for a dollar, dollar, dollar.

The dollar wouldn't spend, spend, spend,
So she threw it in the grass, grass, grass,
Grass wouldn't grow, grow, grow,
So she chopped it with a hoe, hoe, hoe.

Well, the hoe wouldn't chop, chop, chop,
So she took it to the shop, shop, shop,
And the shop made money, money, money,
Like the bees make honey, honey, honey.

Way down yonder, yonder, yonder,
In jailbird town, town, town,
Where the women all work, work, work,
When the sun goes down, down, down.

Sorida

The people of Ghana greet each other with the Shona word "sorida." What a great greeting this hand-clapping song is! Start the clapping pattern slowly until you feel comfortable with it. Then try it faster.

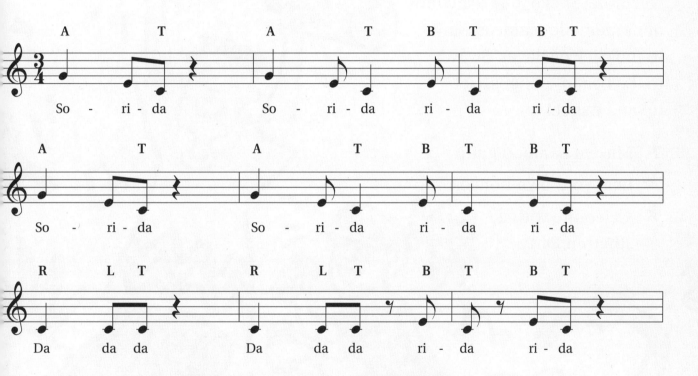

A	T	A	T	B T	B T

So – ri – da   So – ri – da   ri – da   ri – da

A	T	A	T	B T	B T

So – ri – da   So – ri – da   ri – da   ri – da

R	L T	R	L T	B T	B T

Da   da da   Da   da da   ri – da   ri – da

CARNIVAL BAND

It's carnival time — so why not celebrate! Shake to the rhythms of homemade maracas. Sing to the click of claves. Sway to the beat of bongos. Get up and dance!

* Make a bamboo guiro
* Beat your own bongos
* Celebrate with a Rhythm Party

CARNIVAL TIME

Carnival is a time for feasting and kicking up your heels and having fun. It started as a festival celebrated by Roman Catholics before the beginning of Lent — a period of fasting and praying that ends at Easter. The most famous carnival festival is Mardi Gras.

Mardi Gras festivals in New Orleans, Louisiana and Rio de Janeiro, Brazil, feature spectacular parades with fancy floats and lots of loud music. People dress up in wild, colorful costumes and dance in the streets.

Carnival Music

Reggae from Jamaica, calypso from Trinidad, samba from Brazil and rhumba from Cuba — this is carnival music. Carnival musicians play these lively dance rhythms on all kinds of percussion instruments — everything from maracas, guiros, bongos and steel drums to cookie tins, pop cans and trash cans.

Carnival Rhythms

Carnival music uses a strong syncopated rhythm. This means that the stress, or accent of the music falls between the beats. Here th word "and" gets the strongest accent:

1 **and** 2 **and** 3 **and** 4 **and** .

MARACAS

Get your Carnival Band started by making some maracas. Maracas are small hand-held percussion instruments that you shake. Traditionally, they were made of dried gourds with small pebbles or seeds inside. You can make maracas, also called shakers or rattles, from almost any container that you can put beans, seeds or small stones into.

Water Bottle Maracas

A little thirsty from all that dancing? Don't throw out your empty water bottle. Put a teaspoon or two of beans, rice, popcorn or small stones inside it, close the cap and shake.

Film Canister Maracas

Of course, someone will be taking pictures of your carnival, so grab a few empty film canisters before they hit the recycling bin. Put some beans in one and rice in the other. Close the lids and seal them with masking tape. The shaker with the rice will sound lighter than the one with the beans. This difference in tone (or sound quality) comes from the different weight of the rice and beans. Beans are heavier than rice and make a louder sound.

Jingle Loop

Here's a shaker that jingles. If you happen to have a bunch of bottle caps lying around, you're all set to make this jingle loop. If you're not so lucky, you can buy bottle caps at a hardware store.

✳ What You Need

about 100 bottle caps
hole punch
pliers
wire coat hanger
wire cutters
2 corks
colored tape

✳ How You Make It

1 With the hole punch, punch a hole in the center of each bottle cap.

2 Use pliers to undo the twisted neck of the coat hanger. Cut off the twisted end with the wire cutters. Bend the wire into a circle. Put a cork on one end to prevent the caps from falling off.

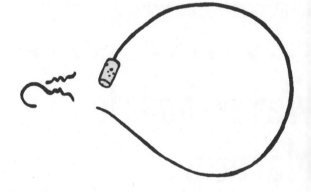

3 Thread the bottle caps onto the wire until it is full but loose enough to jingle. Put a cork on the other end.

4 Twist the two ends together. You may need to use pliers. Remove one cork.

5 Wrap colored tape around the cork end to make a sturdy handle.

Shake It Up!

Get your friends together and make some carnival rhythms by shaking your maracas and jingle loop. Many great carnival songs have a three-beat pattern. To get a feel for this carnival rhythm, count: **1, 2, 3, 1, 2, 3**.

On the first beat, give one maraca a shake: **Shake, 2, 3, shake, 2, 3.** You can also shake on every beat but give a stronger shake (or accent) on the first beat. Like this:

1　**2**　**3**　**1**　**2**　**3**

Shake *shake* *shake* **shake** *shake* *shake*

You can play more than one shaker to add a mixture of tones to the rhythms. Hold a maraca in your left hand and your jingle loop in your right. Shake your maraca on the accented (first) beat and your jingle loop for beats 2 and 3.

GUIROS

The guiro comes from Cuba. It is made from a dried gourd that has ridges or notches cut into it. The guiro player rubs a wooden stick along the ridges in time with the rhythm. Sometimes the guiro is called a scraper.

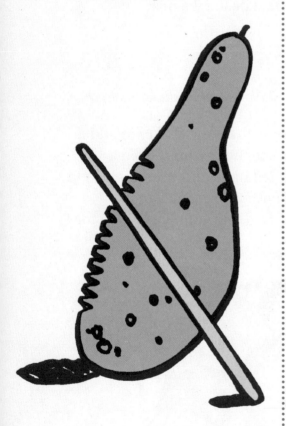

Water Bottle Guiro

Here's another instrument you can make from an empty water bottle. You'll need a plastic bottle that has ridges on the outside. Rub a pencil or chopstick along the ridges.

Cheese Grater Guiro

Check with the head of the household before scraping away on the cheese grater. If you get the go-ahead, try playing it with a heavy plastic comb with long teeth.

Bamboo Guiro

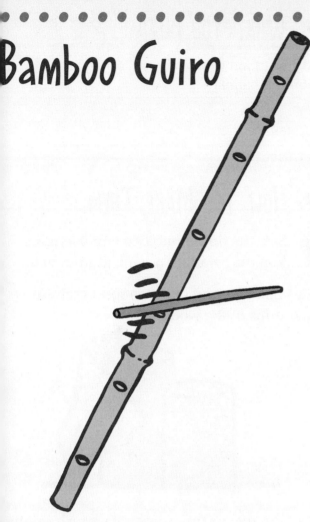

Bamboo may be hard to find in your own backyard, but most garden shops should have some on hand.

☀ WHAT YOU NEED

piece of bamboo, about 30 cm (12 in.) long and .5 cm (1 in.) in diameter

pencil and ruler

nife

wooden dowel or chopstick

☀ HOW YOU MAKE IT

Using your pencil and ruler, mark spots for 6 notches on the bamboo. The notches should all be 5 cm (2 in.) apart. Ask an adult to help you cut the notches with the knife.

☀ HOW YOU PLAY IT

Hold the bamboo stick in one hand. Use the dowel or chopstick to rub along the notches of the scraper.

Cuban Claves

Here's another instrument from Cuba. The claves are two hardwood sticks that are clapped together. Play them to help keep the beat of your carnival rhythms.

✳ WHAT YOU NEED

30 cm (12 in.) wooden dowel, same thickness as a broom handle
saw
sandpaper
varnish

✳ HOW YOU MAKE THEM

1 Saw the dowel into two equal lengths. You may want to ask an adult to help.

2 Use the sand paper to round off the ends of the wood.

3 Put two or three coats of varnish on the sticks. Let them dry between each coat.

✳ HOW YOU PLAY THEM

Cup your hand and rest one of the claves in your fingers. Your hand position is important. If you hold the clave too tight or let it rest against your palm, the sound will be deadened. Cupping your hand lets the sound resonate. Hold the other clave in your free hand and tap the two sticks together.

RHYTHM STICKS

Our earliest ancestors probably made music by tapping two sticks together as they relaxed around the fire. And you probably did the same thing to keep a steady beat in a kindergarten rhythm band. You can make lots of different sounds with just two sticks.

Here a Tap, There a Tap

Find different kinds of wooden sticks — some longer, some thicker — and some made from different kinds of wood. How many different sounds can you make just by tapping these two pieces of wood together? Try tapping the sticks at the end and then at the middle.

How Low Can You Go?

Here's how to get different notes using just a stick. Place a ruler on the table so that 10 cm (4 in.) hangs over the edge. Hold the ruler down firmly against the table with one hand and pluck downward on the end with your other hand. Listen. Next, move the ruler so that it hangs over 15 cm (6 in.). Pluck it again.

The second sound is lower because the length of the ruler hanging over the edge of the table is longer, and the vibrations are moving slower. Try this again using a meter (yard) stick. Let the stick hang way over the table and pluck it. What's the lowest note you can play?

Carpet-Tube Bongos

Visit a carpet store and ask the owner if you can have a few large carpet tubes that might be lying around. They make great drums when you cut them into different lengths. No carpet tubes? Try Sonotubes instead. You can buy them at most large building stores.

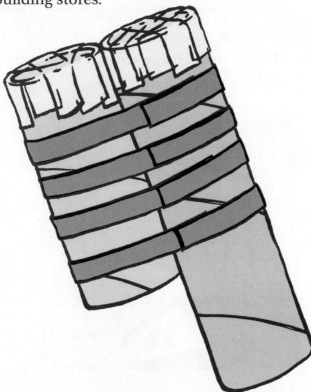

✴ What You Need

2 lengths of carpet tubing 30 cm (12 in.) and 45 cm (18 in.) long
roll of packing tape
colored tape
white glue
piece of cardboard

✴ How You Make Them

1 Ask an adult to cut the tubes to the right length.

2 Crisscross about a dozen layers of packing tape over one end of each tube. This makes the drumheads.

3 Place the tubes side by side on a table with the drumheads facing down and even with each other. Tape them together by putting one row of colored tape near the top and another near the bottom.

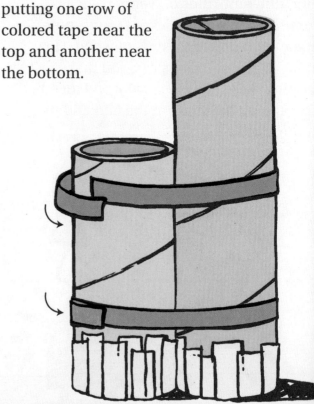

4 Run a line of glue into the seam where the tubes touch on both sides. Push the glue into the seam with a piece of cardboard.

5 Continue to wrap colored tape around the tubes to keep them together.

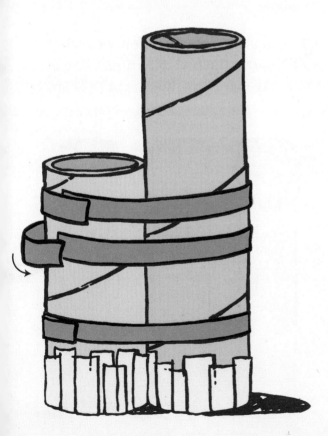

6 Let the glue dry before playing the bongos.

✱ How You Play Them

Sit down and hold the bongos between your knees. Tap the right drumhead with your right hand and the left drumhead with your left hand. Notice how the short tube has a higher sound than the longer tube. Try out some rhythm patterns on your bongos.

Chip-Can Drums

How about making a set of drums that has six drumheads and six different sounds? First, you have to eat your way through six tall cans of potato chips!

✳ WHAT YOU NEED

6 empty chip cans, made of cardboard with plastic lids

ruler and pencil

masking tape

knife

packing tape

✳ HOW YOU MAKE THEM

1 Place the cans top down on a table. Measure up from the plastic lid and mark the spot with a pencil.

Tube 1: 23 cm (9 in.)

Tube 2: 20 cm (8 in.)

Tube 3: 17.5 cm (7 in.)

Tube 4: 15 cm (6 in.)

Tube 5: 12.5 cm (5 in.)

Tube 6: 10 cm (4 in.)

2 Put a strip of masking tape under each mark and run it around the outside of the can. This will give you a straight line to follow.

3 Cut along the straight lines and remove the bottom from each can. (You may want an adult to cut the cans.)

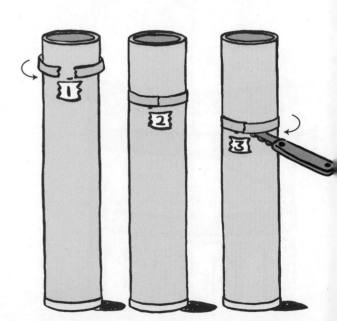

4 Place the tubes top down on a table. Use packing tape to tape them together in pairs — **1** with **2**, **3** with **4**, **5** with **6**. Keep the plastic tops level.

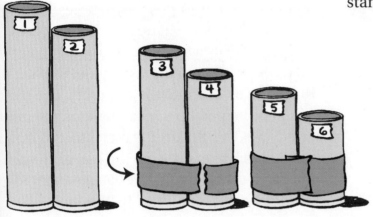

✱ How You Play Them

Sit and hold the cans between your legs. Tap the lids with your hands. The shortest tube makes the highest tone, and the longest tube makes the lowest tone. You can also play standing up.

5 Tape the three sets together in a group so that all the tops are level.

STEEL DRUMS

In Trinidad and the West Indies, oil drums are hammered into instruments that are played like musical drums or gongs. They are called steel drums, and they come in three sizes. The smallest drum, or pan, makes the highest note and is used for playing the melody. The middle-sized pan is the guitar, or rhythm, pan. The largest pan makes a deep bass sound.

It takes a lot of experience to make a steel drum. First, the builder uses a heavy leather mallet to "sink the pan," or pound the top down. Next, shapes are traced with chalk. Each shape produces a different note — a tenor pan, for example, has 28 notes. Then the note shapes are hammered deeper into the pan. The longer shapes make the lower notes. Next, the builder uses a metal cutter to cut the oil drum to the right size. The pan has to be heated up with a blowtorch or put into a fire. This makes the metal soft so that the builder can gently tap the pan until each note is in tune. Finally, the pan gets sent to a factory where it is dipped in chrome.

Coffee-Can Steel Drums

You can make your own version of the steel drum using six coffee cans. That's a lot of coffee!

* What You Need

6 empty coffee cans, all the same size, with tops cut off

hammer

marker

* How You Make Them

1 With a hammer, gently pound the bottoms of the coffee cans so that each one has a different pitch. The can that has the deepest and most dents makes the highest sound. The can with the fewest dents makes the lowest sound.

2 Label the cans from numbers 1 to 6, starting with the lowest-sounding one. Put the lowest-sounding can on your left and the highest-sounding can on your right.

* How You Play Them

Play your steel drums with a stick or pencil held in each hand. Strike the pan several times quickly with both sticks at once. This is called playing a "tremolo." Hit one of your cans with both sticks or two different cans at the same time.

JONKUNNU RHYTHM PARTY

When people from Africa were first brought to Jamaica as slaves, they were given a short holiday at Christmas. They wore masks and costumes and danced in a procession. Today this entertainment is called "jonkunnu." Play these jonkunnu rhythms to get everyone dancing.

Warm Up the Band!

First, everyone in the band plays the same thing at the same time to get used to the patterns. Then one instrument starts. When the first player begins line 2, the second player joins in, starting at line 1. When the second player begins line 2, the third player joins in, starting at line 1. The band will end up playing a round.

✳ MARACAS

	1	2	3	4
Line 1	Sh	sh	sh	sh
Line 2	Sh	sh	sh	sh-sh
Line 3	Sh	sh	sh-sh	sh

✳ GUIRO

	1	2	3	4
Line 1	Rub	rub	rub	rub
Line 2	Rub	rub	rub	rub-rub
Line 3	Rub	rub	rub-rub	rub

✳ CLAVES

	1	2	3	4
Line 1	Clink	clink	clink	clink
Line 2	Clink	clink	clink	clink-clink
Line 3	Clink	clink	clink-clink	clink

TAMBO RHYTHM PARTY

Tambo dancing is a flat-footed dance done in Jamaica. It was brought to the island from Africa and is very similar to dances done in western Nigeria. The drum plays one part, and a higher-pitched instrument plays the other part.

	1	2	3	4
Drum	Goodum	(rest)	goodum	(rest)
Claves	Clink	clink-clink	clink	clink-clink
Drum	Goodum	(rest)	boom-boom	boom-boom
Claves	Clink	clink-clink	clink	clink-clink

Brown Girl in the Ring

Play shakers, guiros and bongos to put this lively singing game in motion. You can hit one instrument on the first beat of every bar, another on just the second beats, and a third on every beat.

1. There's a brown girl in the ring, Tra la la la la, There's a brown girl in the ring, Tra la la la la. There's a brown girl in the ring, Tra la la la la, For she likes sug - ar and I like plum.

2. Skip across the ocean, Tra la la la la,
   Won't you skip across the ocean, Tra la la la la.
   Oh, skip across the ocean, Tra la la la la,
   For she likes sugar and I like plum.

3. Show me your motion, Tra la la la la,
   Won't you show me your motion, Tra la la la la.
   Show me your motion, Tra la la la la,
   For she likes sugar and I like plum.

4. Wheel and spin a partner, Tra la la la la,
   Won't you wheel and spin a partner, Tra la la la la
   Wheel and spin a partner, Tra la la la la,
   For she likes sugar and I like plum.

Marian

Click your claves and jangle your jingle
loop to this light and lively carnival
song. Every bar has four beats. For fun
try keeping the beat on the first and
third beat of every bar.

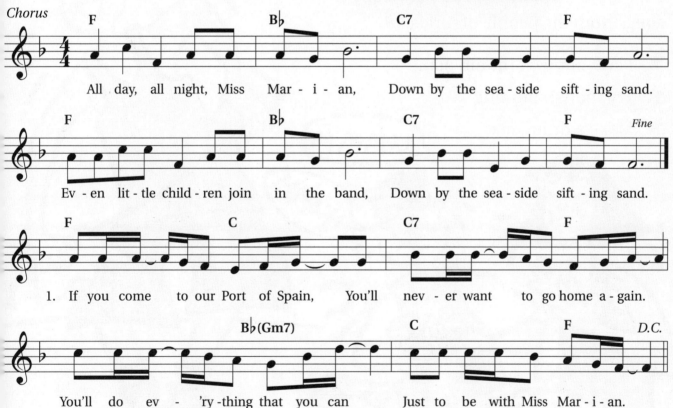

Chorus

All day, all night, Miss Mar - i - an, Down by the sea - side sift - ing sand.

Ev - en lit - tle child - ren join in the band, Down by the sea - side sift - ing sand.

1. If you come to our Port of Spain, You'll nev - er want to go home a - gain.

You'll do ev - 'ry -thing that you can Just to be with Miss Mar - i - an.

2. Our island is so very fine,
Land of hummingbird and sunshine.
You'll agree it's so very nice,
Miss Marian makes it paradise.

3. All the people come to Carnival,
Go and join in the Bacchanal.
Every islander, boy and man,
Want to see Miss Marian.

KALIMBA BAND

The beat of a drum, the twang of a kalimba, the swish of a beaded gourd — this is the music of Africa. You can put together a band with these instruments and play along with songs from the people of Africa.

* Play your own thumb piano
* Try "poly-humming"
* Make a drum talk

♪ **MUSIC NOTES**

Polyrhythmic Music

Polyrhythmic music is music that has two different rhythms performed at the same time. African music often uses a drone (a constant note) with a melody (notes that move up and down) weaving around it.

THE MUSIC OF AFRICA

In most of the popular music we listen to, you can hear a regular beat and rhythm pattern. African music is different. Instead of sticking to one rhythm for a song, the musicians weave together a series of different rhythm patterns.

Usually, there is no conductor leading the group or band. It is up to each player to keep in time with the others. Expert players do not speed up or slow down. They keep the tempo steady. If they didn't, you can imagine the jumble!

Poly-Clapping

To get the feel of African music, try some poly-clapping. Clap these two different lines with a friend to create your own polyrhythm patterns.

	1	2	3	4
Person 1	Clap	clap	(rest)	clap
Person 2	Clap-clap	(rest)	clap-clap	clap

Poly-Humming

Try some poly-humming with a friend. One of you hums a note and holds it for a long time. The other person first hums the same note, then a higher note, then a lower note. Keep trying different notes until you've got harmony (notes that sound good together).

Much More Music

African musicians play many different styles of music. Soukous music of Zaire is dance music played on bass, horns, electric guitars and percussion. The guitar riffs copy the sounds of the kalimba. Lady Blacksmith Mambazo, a popular a capella group from South Africa, performs music that comes from the call-and-response songs of Zulu workers. Juju music of Nigeria uses guitars, banjos and percussion instruments. In songs of praise, the musicians play the talking drum to imitate the sounds of people's voices.

Pop-Can Hosho

In Zimbabwe, the Shona people call a rattle made from a dried gourd a "hosho." They call the sound it makes "chaka," which means "splashing." When you say "chaka, chaka, chaka," the words mimic the swishing, snapping sounds of the hosho rattle.

Swish out some African rhythms with this simple-to-make hosho. While you're at it, why not make two?

✳ WHAT YOU NEED

2 empty pop cans

dried beans

packing tape

✳ HOW YOU MAKE IT

1 Fill the empty, clean pop cans with the dried beans.

2 Completely seal the holes with packing tape.

★ How You Play It

There are no rules about how to shake a hosho. So here's your chance to experiment. First, repeat and play with the word "hosho" until you've got a rhythm you like: **HO**-sho, **HO**-sho, **HO**-sho, **HO**-sho. Now, try these two positions and shake your hosho!

Hold the can in your hand as if you're drinking pop. Then shake it up and down.

Hold the can in the palm of your hand with your palm facing up. Bend your elbow so that the can moves back and forth from your shoulder.

Rattle and Shake!

With two cans, you can make up some fun rhythm patterns like these:
(**R** = rattle in right hand **L** = rattle in left hand)

	1	2	3	4
Pattern 1	R-R	L-L	R-R	L-L
Pattern 2	R	L	R-R	L
Pattern 3	L-R-L	L-R-L	L-R-L	L-R-L

Tin-Can Gankogui Gongs

In Ghana and Zimbabwe, musicians play two bell-shaped gongs, called "gankogui." One bell-gong is bigger than the other. When a musician taps the gongs with a stick, the smaller one makes a higher sound and the bigger one makes a lower sound.

For your Kalimba Band, you can make gankogui gongs from two tin cans.

✳ What You Need

2 empty tin cans, 500 mL (16 oz.) and 650 mL (20 oz.), with label and one end removed
spike
hammer
U-hook with legs about 8 cm (3 in.) apart
4 nuts
colored tape
stick

✳ How You Make Them

1 Use the hammer and spike to poke a hole in the center of each can lid. You may want to ask an adult to help.

2 Screw a nut onto each leg of the U-hook as far as it will go. Place each can on a leg of the U-hook.

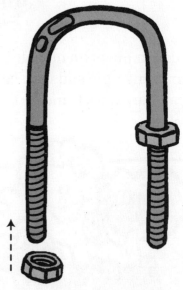

3 Wrap tape around the rough rims of the cans. Screw the other nuts onto the legs of the U-hook, which are now inside the cans. Tighten the outside nuts so the cans are secure.

★ How You Play Them

Hold the U-hook in one hand. With the stick in your other hand, tap one can at a time. Hit the cans on the outside, inside and on the rim. You can muffle the sound by holding one of the cans and then hitting it.

Tin-Can Rhythms

You can make up rhythm patterns by hitting the two bells at different times. Try these.
(**B** = big can   **S** = small can)

	1	2	3	4	1	2	3	4
Pattern 1	B	S	B	S	B	S	B	S
Pattern 2	B-B	S	B-B	S	B-B	S	B-B	S
Pattern 3	S-S	S	B	B	S	S-S	B	S-S

Axatse Shaker

Here's a shaker with the beads on the outside. In Ghana, it's called an axatse. It is made from a dried gourd that has a long neck for a handle. The beads or seashells are strung on cords that form a net on the outside.

Musicians tap the beaded netting to make a sharp, clicking sound. To make a swishing sound, they twist the axatse to make the beaded netting turn around the gourd. To create a thud sound, axatse players hold the axatse in one hand and hit it against the other hand.

✳ WHAT YOU NEED

roundish gourd with a long neck for a handle

plastic cord

scissors

wooden or glass beads

tape

✳ HOW YOU MAKE IT

1 To dry the gourd, put it in an oven overnight at a very low temperature (65°C or 150°F).

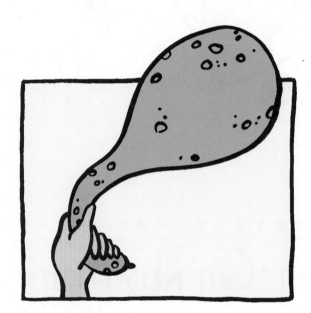

2 Cut 2 short pieces of cord, each about 10 cm (4 in.) long. Then cut 12 pieces of cord, each about twice as long as the gourd.

3 Place one of the short cords on a table and tie it in a circle. Tie the 12 long pieces of cord to the circle so they are evenly spaced.

4 Make a knot in each cord about 2.5 cm (1 in.) down from where it's attached to the circle. String a bead onto the cord up to the knot. Add a knot below the bead to hold it in place. Make another knot about 2.5 cm (1 in.) below the first bead. Add a second bead and knot. Continue until you have five or six beads on each cord.

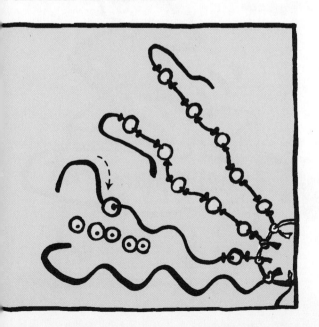

5 Tape the circle cord to the bottom of the gourd. Tie the other short cord around the handle of the gourd. Knot the beaded cords to the handle cord so they are evenly spaced and loose enough to shake.

✳ How You Play It

This gourd gets you up and moving. You can tap it on your knee, shoulder or hips. You can toss it in the air and catch it. You can dance to the swishing, thumping, clicking sounds you make. Here is one way to get to know your axatse:

Pa = a tap on your lap
ti = a tap on the palm of your hand

	1	2	3	4
Pattern 1	Pa-ti-	Pa	Pa-ti-	Pa
Pattern 2	Pa-ti-	Pa-Pa	Pa-ti-	Pa-Pa
Pattern 3	Pa-Pa-	ti	Pa-Pa-	ti

TALKING DRUMS

In parts of Africa, people once sent messages to each other by drumming on giant logs, called slit gongs. Messages could travel as far as 30 km (18 mi.). But only people who spoke the same language as the drummer could understand the message. That's because the drumming patterns imitated the sounds of the drummer's language. When parents wanted to call their children, they would drum the sound of their children's names on the slit gongs.

Making Drum-Talk

If you don't have any logs handy to make slit gongs, use a large cardboard box. Send some messages to your friends by drumming the rhythm of their names on the bottom.

Hello Margaret

Master Drumming

In Africa, a master drummer holds the music together while other drummers play different rhythms and patterns. It takes practice and patience to become a master drummer!

Collect some instruments, get some friends together and try these drumming patterns. Here's a hint: When counting out the rhythm, say "and" between each beat.

Count	1	and	2	and	3	and	4	and	5	and	6	and
Master drummer	Toom		toom		toom		toom		toom		toom	
Count	1	and	2	and	3	and	4	and	5	and	6	and
Axatse	Tap-	tap	tap			tap-	tap	tap			tap-	tap	tap
Count	1	and	2	and	3	and	4	and	5	and	6	and
Hosho		Ch		ch		ch		ch		ch		ch
Count	1	and	2	and	3	and	4	and	5	and	6	and
Bass drum		Bam!					Bam!		Bam-	bam	bam!	
Count	1	and	2	and	3	and	4	and	5	and	6	and
Gangkogui	Ding-	ga	ding			ding-	ga	ding			ding-	ga	ding

Tin-Can Friction Drum

The friction drum is a popular instrument in Zambia. It has a stick that goes through the middle of the skin that is stretched across the top. When a musician moves the stick up and down, it rubs against the skin and this friction creates musical vibrations.

Make your own friction drum from an old tin can. It will keep a good scratchy rhythm. It might even bark!

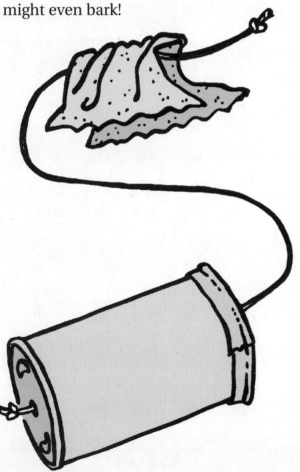

* WHAT YOU NEED

tin can 369 g (13 oz.), one end removed

masking tape

hammer and nail

piece of string 43 cm (17 in.) long

paper towel

* HOW YOU MAKE IT

1 Put tape around the open rim of the can to cover any rough edges.

2 Use the hammer and nail to poke a hole in the bottom of the can.

3 Feed string through the hole from the outside. Reach inside and pull the string halfway through.

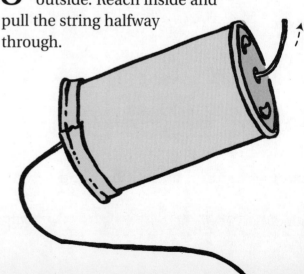

4 Make a knot at each end of the string. Pull the string all the way through to the knot.

* How You Play It

Hold the can under one arm, open end down. Take a damp paper towel in your other hand and reach inside the can and grab the string near the hole. Pull down on the string to make a sound.

ROAR

Paper-Cup Friction Drum

Next time you finish a take-out drink, don't throw away that paper cup with its plastic lid and straw. You can turn it into a friction drum. Pull up and down on the straw so that it rubs against the lid. This causes the lid to vibrate and make a high-pitched, scratching sound.

Popsicle-Stick Kalimba

The kalimba is sometimes called a thumb piano because you can play it with just your thumbs! In Zimbabwe, kalimbas are made from a dried gourd and metal tongs of different lengths. Here's a kalimba you can make with some leftover wood and a few Popsicle sticks.

✳ WHAT YOU NEED

small piece of hardwood, 2 cm wide x 0.5 cm thick x 12 cm long (¾ in. x ¼ in. x 4¾ in.)

drill and 0.5 cm (³⁄₁₆ in.) drill bit

sandpaper

piece of 1 x 6 wood for the soundboard, 14 cm (5½ in.) long

awl

hammer

soap or wax

3 number 8 screws, 2 cm (¾ in.) long

screwdriver

5 Popsicle sticks

dowel 14 cm (5 ½ in.) long and 0.5 cm (¼ in.) thick

✳ HOW YOU MAKE IT

1 Use the small piece of wood to make the bridge. Drill three holes in the bridge, one in the center and one at each end, about 1.5 (½ in.) from the end. (You may want adult help with this step.) Use the sandpaper to smooth any rough spots.

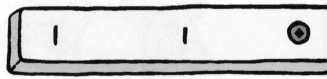

2 Place the bridge on top of the large piece of wood (the soundboard), leaving about 2.5 cm (1 in.) at the top. Using the awl, mark the three spots for the drilled holes on the soundboard. Remove the bridge.

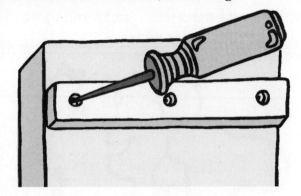

3 With the awl and hammer, make the holes in the soundboard a bit larger. Sand any rough edges.

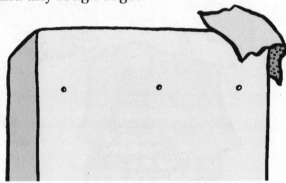

4 Rub soap or wax on the screws. Screw the bridge loosely to the soundboard.

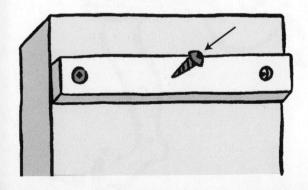

5 Insert the Popsicle sticks under the bridge.

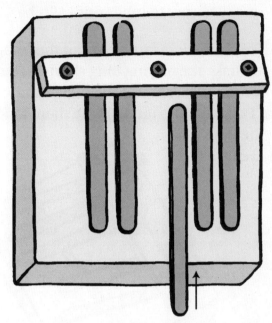

6 Slip the dowel under the sticks and move it up close to the bridge.

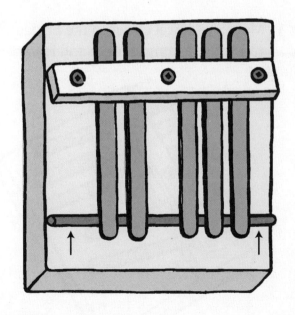

✱ HOW YOU TUNE IT

Here are two ways to tune your kalimba.

1 Push the sticks farther under the bridge to make the playing tong shorter. The shorter the stick, or tong, the higher the note. Pull the tongs out to make them longer, and the note will be lower.

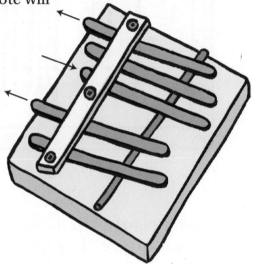

2 Move the dowel closer to the bridge to make the tongs longer and lower in pitch.

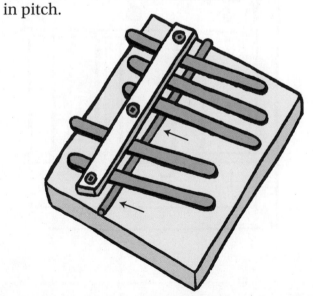

✱ HOW YOU PLAY IT

Cradle the kalimba in both hands so that your thumbs are free to pluck the tongs. Expert players pluck the tongs downward with the right and left thumbs and upward with the right index finger.

Kalimba Rhythms

Now try some kalimba rhythms! The right thumb plucks the center tong and the two tongs to the right. The left thumb plucks the two tongs on the left.

1L = first tong left of center, left thumb

2L = second tong left of center, left thumb

R = center tong, right thumb

1R = first tong right of center, right thumb

2R = second tong right of center, right thumb

1	2	3	4	5
Tong	*tong*	*tong*	*tong*	*tong*
2L	1L	R	1R	2R

Try playing a different rhythm pattern with each thumb at the same time.

	1	2	3	4
Right thumb	R	1R		2R
Left thumb	1L		2L	

Congo Lullaby

You can keep a steady beat to this lullaby by clapping your hands or playing the hosho, gankogui or axatse. Every bar has two beats. You can play on every beat or only on the second beat of each bar.

Tune your thumb piano to a five-note pentatonic scale with the notes C,D,E,G,A. Pluck the tongs with your thumbs while singing the song. "Ta-ta" means father and "ba-ta" means duck.

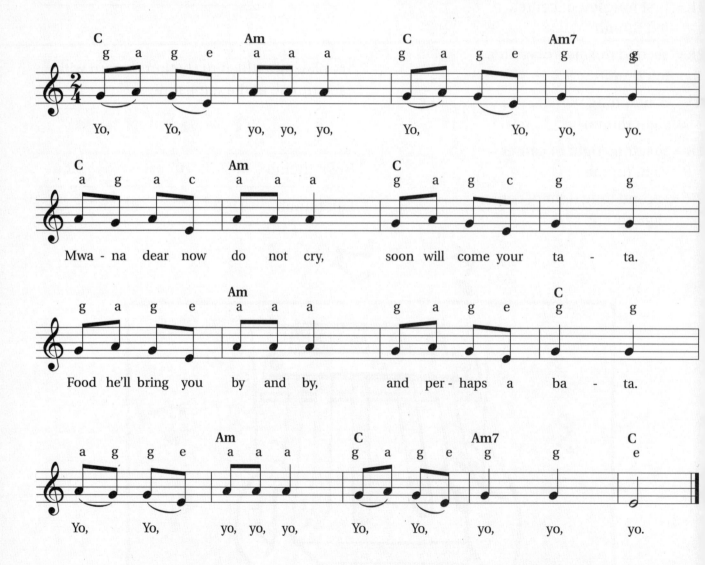

Chawe Chidyo Chem'chero

This song comes from a story told by the Shona people of Ghana and Zimbabwe. One day a kudu sneaks into a family's fields. Everyone tries to scare the kudu away by clanging pots, throwing things and chasing it. But nothing works. The kudu is smart. It knows it can continue chomping on the crops if it casts a spell over the people by singing this song.

The song has two parts. Learn one at a time by having one person lead and everyone else echo back. Once both parts have been learned, divide the group into two sections. Each section sings their part over and over again.

This song has four beats to a bar. Try this rhythm pattern for the song by clapping or playing an instrument:

STRING BAND

The jiggedy jig of the cornstalk fiddle and the plinkety plunk of the jug banjo — this is country music from the mountains to the plains. Rosin up your bow, kick up your heels and get ready to play some good old country tunes.

* Make a cornstalk fiddle
* Play the spoons
* Learn how to yodel

 **Sound Bites**

Ancient Strings

People have been making music with strings since prehistoric times. Archaeologists discovered a cave painting in southern France that shows a hunter playing a mouth bow as he stalks a pair of bison. The painting is probably 18 000 years old.

STRING MUSIC

The roots of country music arrived in the eastern United States about 200 years ago. The Scottish and English immigrants who settled along the Appalachian Mountains played their traditional folk songs on the simple string instruments — fiddles, banjos and guitars. They also made their own string instruments from materials they had on hand, such as the cornstalk fiddle and the jug banjo. Their unique style of music spread across the continent from one musician to another. New elements were added, and country and western music was born.

String Vibrations

When a string is held tight and plucked, strummed or bowed, it vibrates and produces a sound. The pitch of the sound depends on the length of the string, what the string is made of and how tightly it is stretched. The longer the string, the lower the sound.

You can test this out with a string experiment. You'll need a sturdy frame to string your string on, something that has a long and a short side — such as a rectangular box or baking pan. First, attach a string (or elastic) to the long side. Pluck it and listen. Now, attach it to the short side and pluck again. The longer string makes a lower sound because it vibrates more slowly than the short string. A shorter string produces faster vibrations and a higher pitch.

Harps and Lyres

The harp is one of the oldest string instruments. Each string of a harp is a different length and produces its own note.

The lyre was the favorite string instrument of the ancient Greeks. With fewer strings than the harp, a musician could play more notes by pressing on a string to shorten its vibrations and raise its pitch.

One-String Mouth Bow

Appalachian settlers probably borrowed the idea for this instrument from Native American musicians, who played the mouth bow for celebrations and ceremonies.

* What You Need

wooden meter (yard) stick, or similar length of wood that is long, strong and flexible

saw or craft knife

guitar string

wire cutters

rubber washer

tape

* How You Make It

1 Saw or cut a 1.5 cm (½ in.) V-shaped notch in each end of the stick.

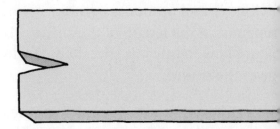

2 Cut two more smaller notches on the sides of one end of the stick, 2.5 cm (1 in.) down.

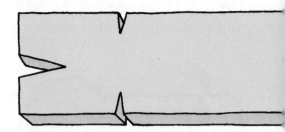

3 Loop the thin end of the guitar string around the side notches and bring it up and through the end notch. Wrap the wire securely and snip off the end with wire cutters.

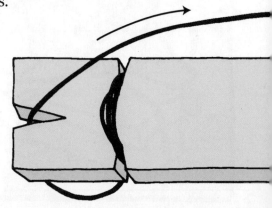

4 Slip the rubber washer over the knob of the other end of the string. Wrap tape around the metal knob of the string until it is too thick to slip through the washer.

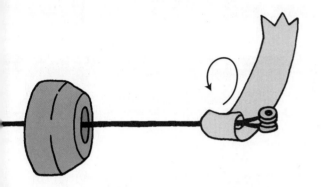

5 Place the end of the stick with the three notches on the floor. Bend the stick. Place the washer end of the string over the other notched end.

Hold one end of the bow against your cheek and lips. Pluck the string with your fingers, a guitar pick or a seashell. As you pluck the string, change the shape of your mouth and move your tongue. This makes a faint melody that you can control. Practice keeping a steady rhythm by plucking back and forth patterns. Gradually increase the speed. If you want to sit and play, place the end of the bow on your knee and bend the stick to change the pitch.

• • • • • • • • • • • • •

Cornstalk Fiddle

Your cornstalk fiddle won't be perfectly in tune, but it's still fun to make and play.

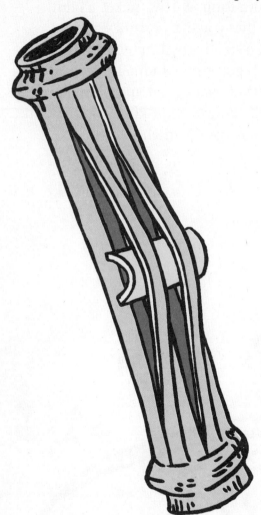

✳ What You Need

dry cornstalk

sharp craft knife

rosin

✳ How You Make It

1 Cut the cornstalk above and below two joints, or nodes, so that you have a long, strong section.

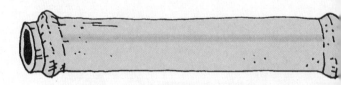

2 Notice the groove running down one side of the stalk. Using your craft knife, carefully make two cuts on each side of the groove, from joint to joint. These cuts make the "strings" of your fiddle. They need to be wide enough so they won't break.

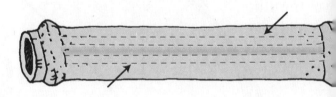

3 Cut a small piece from the remaining stalk. Slice it in half, and carefully insert it under the string to make a bridge.

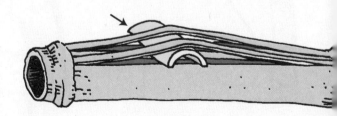

A Bow for Your Fiddle

When you pull and push a bow across a fiddle, the notes last longer than they would if you just plucked the strings. You can make a fiddle bow using a twig and following the instructions for the mouth bow. Use strong cotton thread instead of the guitar string. Rub some rosin along the string so that the bow moves easily over the strings of your fiddle. Rosin, which looks like a golden chunk of candy, is made out of the sap from pine trees. You can buy it at a music store.

Fiddling Fun

You can play your cornstalk fiddle with your twig bow — or try making a cornstalk bow. Hold the fiddle up to your collar bone. Take the bow in your other hand and draw it very gently back and forth across the strings. To change the pitch, hold the string down with your fingers. The note will be higher. Now, play along to the chorus of "Cornstalk Fiddle and a Shoe String Bow" (page 184). Try following just the rhythm of the words as you pluck or bow your fiddle:

I made me a fiddle and I made me a bow,

And I learned to play like Cotton Eye Joe.

ANATOMY OF A GUITAR

You can't have country music without the great sounds of a guitar! The first guitar was probably played in Europe in the 14th century. Eventually, it replaced the lute as the most popular instrument in the home for accompanying family singalongs.

Tuning Pegs

These are small pegs attached to the strings at the end of the neck. A peg can tighten a string to raise its pitch or loosen a string to lower its pitch.

Frets

These are raised ridges (or bridges) that are fixed to the neck. They are set out in exact measurements so that musicians can shorten or lengthen the strings to play the right notes.

Sound Box

When you strum the guitar strings, they vibrate and the vibrations travel through the bridge and into the hollow sound box. This makes the whole box vibrate.

Bridge

A bridge is a piece of wood, plastic or other material that is placed under strings to keep them up off of the fingerboard or neck of the instrument. This allows the strings to vibrate freely.

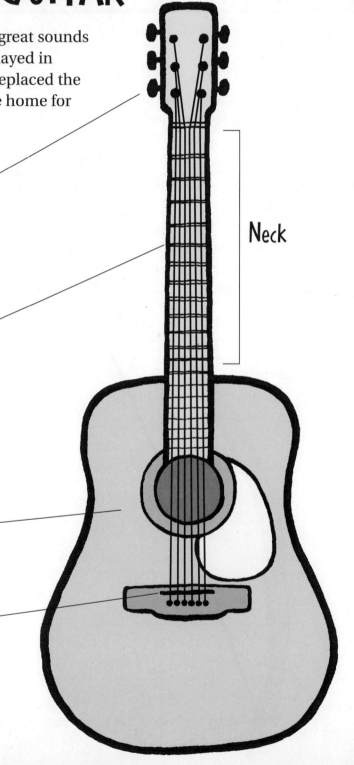

Neck

How to Play a Guitar

Hold the strings down to the fingerboard with the fingers of your left hand (if you are right-handed). By placing your fingers on a string between the frets, you can shorten the string or lengthen it. If you move your fingers closer to the body of the guitar, the string will be shorter and the note higher.

Use your fingers on your other hand to pluck or strum the strings.

Guitar Chords

The numbers on the charts below indicate the fingering. An empty circle indicates optional fingering. A broken line indicates that a string should not be played; a solid line with no fingering indicates that a string should be played open. (For more chords, see page 205.)

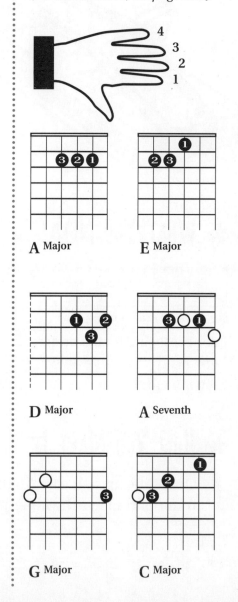

A **Major**   E **Major**

D **Major**   A **Seventh**

G **Major**   C **Major**

Match-Box Guitar

This tiny homemade guitar fits right into your pocket so you can take it anywhere.

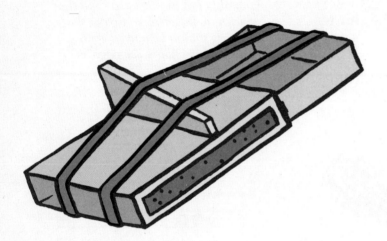

✱ What You Need

empty match box

white glue

scissors or craft knife

thick cardboard for the bridge, same width as the matchbox

rubber bands

✱ How You Make It

1 Open the box half way. Mark where the outer part meets the inner part.

2 Remove the inner part. Put glue on the sides and the bottom up to the mark.

3 Insert the inner part into the outer part. Let the glue dry.

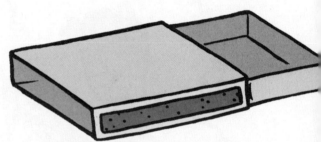

4 Use scissors or a craft knife to cut out the bridge. The bridge needs to be the same width as the match box and higher at one end than the other.

5 Stretch two or three rubber bands along the length of the match box.

6 Insert the bridge under the rubber bands.

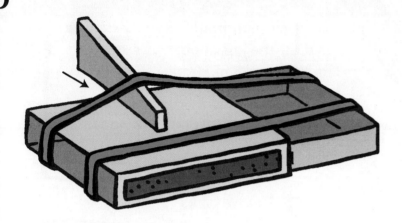

✳ How You Play It

Hold your guitar in one hand and pluck or strum it with the fingers of the other. To make a higher sound or note, pull one rubber band tighter. Try to get a different note from each rubber-band string.

Pluck and Strum

Plucking is pulling up or down on one string at a time with the fingers, thumb or a pick.

pluck

Strumming is playing all the strings at the same time with your thumb or fingers or with a flat pick. Strum both up and down across the strings.

strum

Jug Banjo

What would a down home country band be without the plinketty-plonketty sound of a banjo?

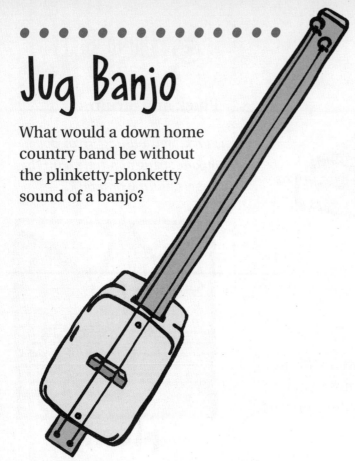

✱ What You Need

4-litre (1 gallon) plastic jug with a flat bottom for the sound box

large pair of scissors

piece of wood for the fingerboard, 75 cm long, 3 cm wide, 2 cm thick (30 in. x 1¼ in. x ¾ in.)

4 upholstery tacks

2 guitar strings

hammer

large nail

2 screw eyes

small piece of wood for the bridge, about 5 cm x 1 cm x 1 cm (2 in. x ½ in. x ½ in.)

craft knife

glue

✱ How You Make It

1 Cut around the jug, about 12.5 cm (5 in.) from the bottom.

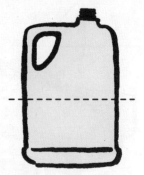

2 Cut two slots about 4.5 cm (1¾ in.) wide on opposite sides of the jug, close to the bottom.

3 Slide the fingerboard through the slots in the jug. The short end should stick out 4 cm (1½ in.). Use two tacks to attach the jug to the fingerboard.

4 Put the third and fourth tacks through the button ends of the guitar strings. Hammer them to the short end of the fingerboard, about 2.5 cm (1 in.) apart.

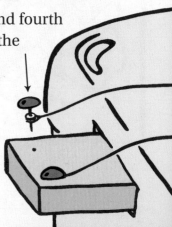

5 Use a hammer and nail to make two holes at the long end of the fingerboard — one 2.5 cm (1 in.) from the end and the other 5 cm (2 in.) from the end. They should be the same distance apart as the tacks at the short end, about 2.5 cm (1 in.). Screw the screw eyes into the holes.

6 Pull the strings tight and wrap them around the screw eyes. If the screw eyes are too hard to turn, insert the large nail through the holes and turn until the strings are tight.

7 To make the bridge, use the craft knife to cut two grooves in the small piece of wood, 2.5 cm (1 in.) apart.

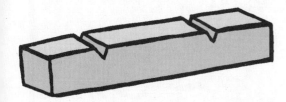

8 Glue the bridge in the center of the sound box and place the strings in the grooves.

★ HOW YOU PLAY IT

Hold the banjo so that your left hand (if you're right-handed) is at the fingerboard and your right hand is at the sound box. The left hand changes the pitch of the strings by holding them down, one at a time or both together. The right hand strums or plucks the strings.

Use a piano or pitch pipe to tune your banjo so one string is tuned to C and the other string to G. You can also tune your banjo so that both strings play the same note. Pluck one string and leave the other one open so that it makes a steady droning tone.

Snappy Spoons

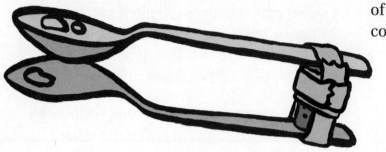

To add some snappy rhythm to your String Band, grab a pair of spoons and let them clack back to back. Raid the kitchen drawer and try out spoons of silver, aluminum, stainless steel and wood. Each set makes a different tone depending on the size and material.

* WHAT YOU NEED

2 spoons that fit into your hands

cork from a wine or vinegar bottle

masking tape

* HOW YOU MAKE THEM

1 Hold the cups of the spoons back to back in one hand.

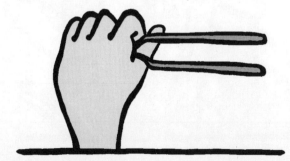

2 Place the cork between the end of the tails of the spoons. Wrap the masking tape over and around the cork and tails of the spoons so that it is very secure. Keep a space of 1–2 cm (½ in.– ¾ in.) at the cup end of the spoons so the cups can clap. (Cut the cork if necessary.)

* HOW YOU PLAY THEM

Hold the tail end of the spoons with one hand so that the cup ends of the spoons are loose. Tap the spoons against your knee. Practice keeping a steady beat.

Tap the spoons in a flat hand, then a cupped hand. Tap the spoons on your shoulders, arms and your partner's back! Each surface gives the spoons a different tone. Some surfaces sound crisp and some sound muffled.

Spoon Skills

Musicians who play the spoons in country and string bands get great rhythms out of just a pair of spoons. Here are some of their spooning techniques.

✳ Ride 'Em Up and Down

Hold the tail of the spoons in one hand and place the other hand a few inches above your knee. On the down stroke, tap your knee. On the up stroke, tap your hand. Start with a slow, steady rhythm, then speed it up!

✳ The Trill

Hold the tail of the spoons in one hand and stiffly fan the fingers of your other hand above your knee. Run the spoons down your fingers and let the spoons land on your knee. You've got it right when your spoon playing sounds like a drumroll in a marching band.

✳ The Tickle

Hold the tail of the spoons in one hand and place the cups near your knee. With the other hand, drum your fingers one at a time up against the cup of the spoon facing your knee. Then let the spoons tap your knee. This should sound similar to The Trill.

YODELLING

People have been yodelling for hundreds of years. The Germans yodel, the Swiss yodel, and some people in Africa yodel. And, of course, country singers yodel.

When yodellers yodel, their voices move quickly from a very low chest sound to a high head sound, or falsetto. It is a little like trying to harmonize with yourself.

Learning how to yodel is as easy as singing "Yo-de-lay-ee-o." Give your vocal chords a work out with this yodel:

Little-o-de-lay-ee-tee

Yo-de-lay-ee, little-o-de-lay-ee-tee

You can make up your own yodels. Just change the vowel sounds in "Yo-de-lay-ee-ee."

BAND PRACTICE

Get your String Band friends together and practice some good old country music! One person sets up a clickety-clack rhythm with the spoons. Two or three yodellers in the band start singing the great old yodelling song, "When Grandma Slid Down the Mountain," just following the rhythm of the words. And the band's best guitarist plays the match-box guitar, plucking on the accented words of the yodellers.

* When Grandma Slid Down the Mountain

When we lived on the mountain,
it was hard to get around

We had to go on down the road,
and that went 'round and 'round

Grandma had a better way,
that of getting down

She'd go on to the mail chute and
slide right into town

Chorus

She slid down the mountain
on her little-o-de-lay-ee-tee

Her little-o-de-lay-ee-tee,
her little-o-de-lay-ee-tee

She slid down the mountain
on her little-o-de-lay-ee-tee

Yo-de-lay-ee, little-o-de-lay-ee-tee.

184

Cornstalk Fiddle and a Shoe String Bow

This tune celebrates the corn fiddle. Play your corn fiddle along to the natural rhythm of the words. A friend can play the mouth bow by plucking it on beat 1 and beat 3 of each bar.

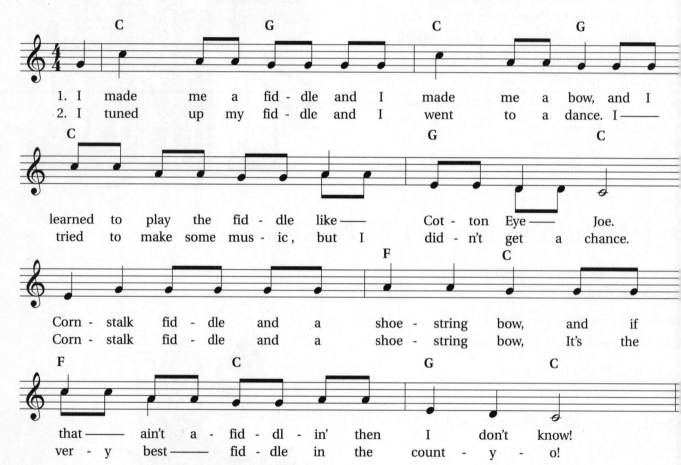

1. I made me a fiddle and I made me a bow, and I
2. I tuned up my fiddle and I went to a dance. I —

learned to play the fiddle like —— Cotton Eye —— Joe.
tried to make some music, but I didn't get a chance.

Corn - stalk fid - dle and a shoe - string bow, and if
Corn - stalk fid - dle and a shoe - string bow, It's the

that —— ain't a fid - dl - in' then I don't know!
ver - y best —— fid - dle in the count - y - o!

3. Cotton Eye Joe lived 'cross the creek.
He learned to play the fiddle 'bout seven days a week.
Cornstalk fiddle and a shoe string bow,
And if that ain't a fiddlin' then I don't know!

4. I've made lots of fiddles and I made lots of bows,
But I never learned to fiddle like Cotton Eye Joe!
Cornstalk fiddle and a shoe string bow,
It's the very best fiddle in the county-o!

Mister Banjo

"Mister Banjo" is a Creole song. Creole people are descendants of the first French settlers in Louisiana.

Pick up your banjo, and strut up and down like the millionaire in the song.

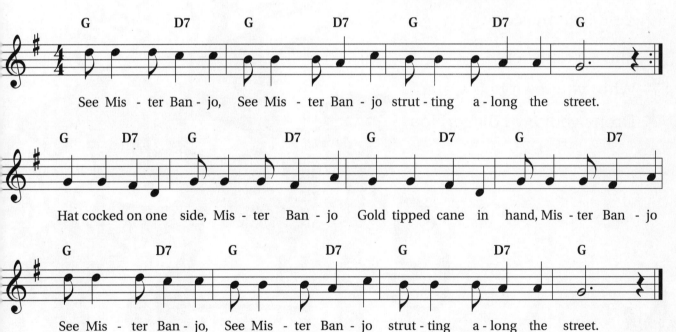

See Mis - ter Ban - jo, See Mis - ter Ban - jo strut - ting a - long the street.

Hat cocked on one side, Mis - ter Ban - jo Gold tipped cane in hand, Mis - ter Ban - jo

See Mis - ter Ban - jo, See Mis - ter Ban - jo strut - ting a - long the street.

WORLD BEAT BAND

Imagine a stick that sounds like rain, a string that roars like thunder and a tube that croaks like a frog. These are the instruments of the people of the deserts, the rainforests and the islands. This is world beat music.

* Make a rainstick
* Whirl your own bull roarer
* Drone your own didgeridoo

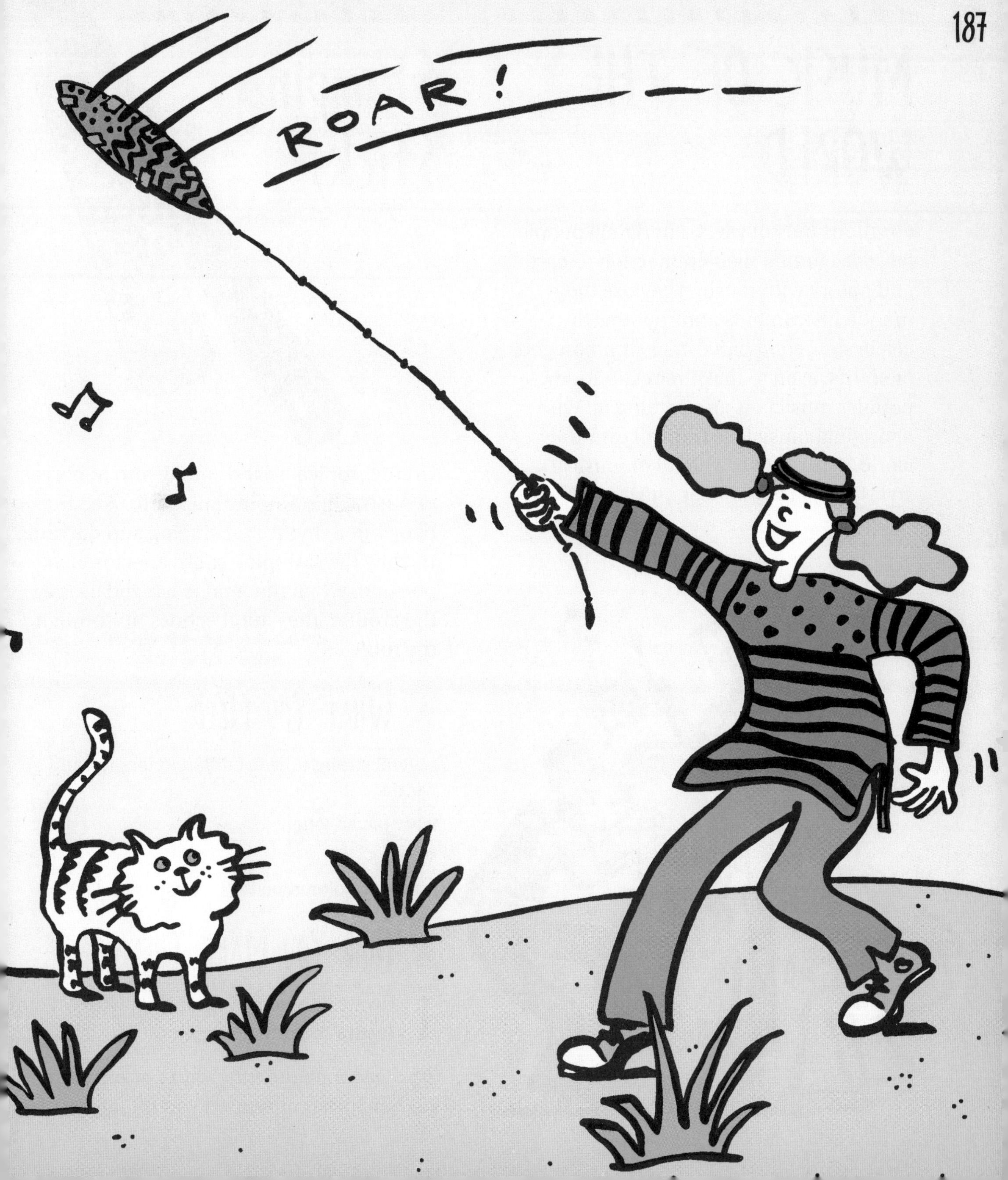
ROAR!

MUSIC OF THE WORLD

For thousands of years, aboriginal people have celebrated their connection to earth and nature with music. They use their unique instruments and rhythms to celebrate a good harvest, to summon gods or spirits, even to make rain fall. Today, popular musicians are teaming up with aboriginal musicians from all over the world. The result is a blend of musical styles we call world beat music.

Stamping Sticks

On the tropical islands of Fiji and in parts of Australia, stamping sticks are used to bang out a rhythm for singing and dancing. Usually the stamping sticks are closed at one end. When that end is banged against the ground, the sound echoes up through the tube.

✳ WHAT YOU NEED

several strong tubes of different lengths and widths

wide packing tape

scissors

markers, colored pencils, or paper and glue

✳ HOW YOU MAKE THEM

1 Cover one end of each tube with several layers of packing tape.

2 Decorate the tube with patterns and shapes that remind you of nature.

* How You Play Them

Experiment by banging the tubes on different surfaces. How do they sound on earth, cement, wood?

STAMP

* Rhythm Game 1

Make up a simple rhythm pattern. You lead and everyone echoes what you play:

	1	2	3	4
Leader	*Bang*	*bang*	*b-b-b-b*	*bang*
Echo	*Bang*	*bang*	*b-b-b-b*	*bang*

* Rhythm Game 2

You lead and everyone responds with a different pattern:

	1	2	3	4
Leader	*Bang*	*bang*	*b-b-b-b*	*bang*
Echo	*B-b-b-b*	*bang*	*bang*	*bang*

* Rhythm Game 3

Everyone plays a simple rhythm pattern that can be repeated over and over. Then, one at a time, each player creates a different pattern that fits in, while the other musicians keep repeating the original pattern. Each player gets to perform alone, or play a solo. Try this:

	1	2	3	4
Group	‖: *Bang*	*bang*	*b-b-b-b*	*bang* :‖
Solo	—— *b-*	*bang*	*bang*	*(rest)*

Bull Roarer

Many instruments from aboriginal cultures mimic the sounds of nature. When the bull roarer is whirled through the air, it sounds like thunder. Its eerie, whooshing sound might even scare bad spirits away.

* What You Need

2 flaps from a cardboard box 30 cm (12 in.) long
pencil
scissors
tape
thick rubber bands

* How You Make It

1 On one flap of cardboard, draw a long oval shape about 30 cm (12 in.) long and 6 cm (2 ½ in.) wide. Cut it out.

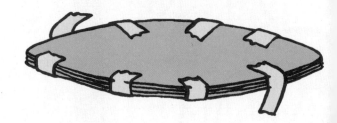

2 Trace the oval shape onto the cardboard two more times. Cut out the ovals.

3 Pile the ovals on top of one another and tape them together to make a disc.

4 With the pointed end of the scissors, poke a hole through the disc about 2 cm (¾ in.) from one end. You may want to ask an adult to help.

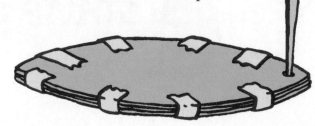

5 Make a chain of rubber bands about 80 cm (32 in.) long. To make the chain, lay the end of one rubber band over the end of another rubber band. This makes a small hole. Loop the tail of the bottom rubber band through the hole and pull it back tightly.

6 Push the tip of the last rubber band through the hole of the disc so that a small loop is formed. Take the tail of the chain and thread it through the loop. Pull the chain all the way through until the chain is snugly fastened.

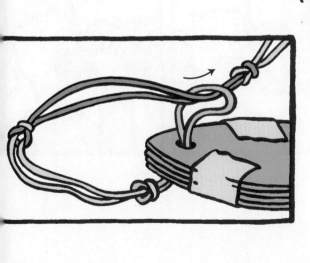

Give yourself plenty of room. Hold on to the rubber-band chain as tight as you can and whirl the disc around your head with every ounce of your muscle power! Eventually, as you whirl the chain above your head the disc will start to spin. Then you will hear the bull roar.

Your bull roarer works like the blades of a helicopter. As the disc whirls and spins through the air, it pushes against the air molecules and causes them to vibrate. These vibrations are the sound waves that you hear.

Didgeridoo

The didgeridoo is an ancient instrument of the aboriginal people of northern Australia. It is traditionally made from the branch of a eucalyptus tree that has been hollowed out by termites. This wind tube is decorated with totems of animals and other things found in nature. The musician plays quiet rhythm patterns by humming and blowing into the tube at the same time.

To make your own didgeridoo, find a tube that is 1.5 m (3 to 5 ft.) long and made of sturdy cardboard or plastic. Try plastic tubes used for storing golf clubs — the rounded end makes a good mouthpiece.

Drone Your Own

The didgeridoo is like a trumpet. You make a sound by blowing a rude noise into the mouthpiece at one end of the tube. When your lips vibrate, the air going into the didgeridoo makes a humming or buzzing sort of drone. You can use your lips, tongue and breathing to change the tone of the drone.

✳ Let It Blow

Relax your lips and let out a burst of air. Do this again as you gently press your lips against the mouthpiece of the tube. Keep your lips loose for low notes and tighter for high notes. If you have a long tube, the sound will be lower than for a shorter tube.

☀ BELLY LAUGHS

Put your hands on your belly and give a huge "ha, ha, ha." Feel the laugh tug in and out just above your belly. Try this while blowing into your didgeridoo. Fill your lungs with air. As you blow the drone, give a belly laugh at the same time.

☀ ANIMAL CALLS

While blowing a drone, you can imitate animal sounds with your didgeridoo. Try "woof, woof" or "croak, croak." You can sing, yap or yowl all you like! Australian aboriginal people copy the donkey-like laugh of the kookaburra.

☀ WAG YOUR TONGUE

One way to drone a rhythm is to move your tongue. Try "tu-tu-tu-tu," "te-te-te-te," "da-da-da-da," "ta-ta-ta-ta" or "ka-ka-ka-ka." When you put some of these sounds together, you can come up with all sorts of interesting rhythms, such as "kakata ta-ta tu-tu" or "da-da kaka da-da."

☀ CIRCULAR BREATHING

When you listen to a didgeridoo, it sounds as if the player never takes a breath. But the player is doing something called circular breathing. Try it. Fill your cheeks with air and keep them puffed out. This extra air makes the drone. At the same time, take a quick breath of air through your nose to top up your lungs. (Quite the trick!)

Rainstick

With a rainstick, you can enjoy the sound of the rain without getting wet. Different forms of rainsticks have been found in China, Africa and South America. Some are made from cactus branches or bamboo. According to aboriginal myths and stories, playing the rainstick reminded the spirits to send down some rain.

Traditional South American rainstick makers have a deep respect for all living things. They will not destroy a living cactus to make their rainsticks. Instead, they look for dead and dried-out pieces of cactus. Small pebbles placed inside the cactus branch ripple over the thorns. It sounds just like rain.

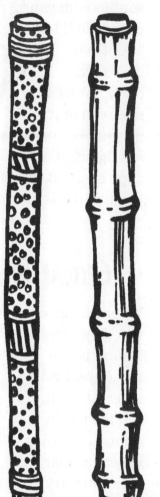

* WHAT YOU NEED

sturdy cardboard tube, at least 46 cm (18 in.) long

packing tape

hobby wire

ruler

125 mL (1/2 cup) rice or dried beans

colored paper, feathers, stickers and paints or markers for decorating

* HOW YOU MAKE IT

1 Seal one end of the tube with several layers of packing tape.

2 Crumple the wire to make several balls. Use a ruler to push them down into the tube until it is full.

3 Pour rice into the tube.

4 Seal the open end of the tube with the packing tape.

5 Decorate your rainstick.

✲ How You Play It

Slowly tip the tube back and forth and let the rice cascade over the balls of hobby wire inside your tube. Close your eyes and listen to the sound of the rain.

Laced Drum

For many aboriginal people of North America, the drum is sacred. Some say the drumbeat is "the heartbeat of a nation and the sound of the universe."

For the drumhead of your laced drum, use chamois, which is sheepskin cured in cod oil. You may also use plain leather.

✳ What You Need

large piece of chamois

large coffee can, both ends removed

pencil

scissors

hole punch

leather lace or gimp

✳ How You Make It

1 Fold the chamois in half. Place the coffee can on top of the chamois and trace a circle about 10 cm (4 in.) bigger all the way around than the can. Cut out the two circles.

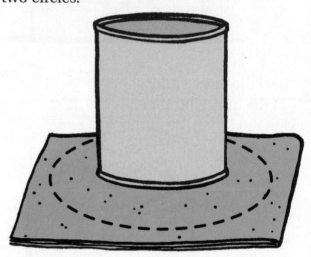

2 Using the hole punch, make 12 evenly spaced holes around the outside of each circle, about 2.5 cm (1 in.) from the edge.

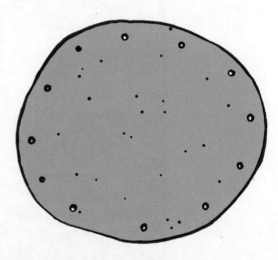

3 Soak the chamois circles in icy cold water for about 30 minutes.

4 Place one wet chamois on a table. Center the can on the top. Center the other wet chamois on the top of the can. Thread the leather lace through every other hole in a zigzag pattern. Pull as tight as you can. When you have finished, tie the ends of the lace together.

5 Allow the drum to dry for 24 hours so that the chamois shrinks.

✳ HOW YOU PLAY IT

You can beat the drum with a homemade drumstick (wooden spoon or dowel) or with your hands. You might want to start by playing softly and gradually getting louder. The heartbeat pattern is played like this:

①	②	①	②
Tap-**tap**	(rest)	tap-**tap**	(rest)

The dance beat is steady. Try it slow, then faster.

①	②	③	④	①	②	③	④
Tap	tap	tap	tap	**tap**	tap	tap	tap

Membranophones

Drums are membranophones, the kind of percussion instruments that have stretched skins that you hit to make the sound. The drum skin is stretched over the body of the drum and held in place with ropes, glue, rings or pegs, and sinew. Aboriginal people used animal skins for drumheads. Your favorite rock group is probably drumming on Mylar, a plastic skin. When you hit the drum skin, you create vibrations that resonate into the body of the drum. The bigger the body, the bigger and deeper the sound.

EARTH CHANT

In their music, aboriginal people express the special respect and gratitude they feel for earth and nature. It is important for all of us to give thanks. Think about the air we breathe, the sun that warms us in the day, the food we eat and the water we drink. Remember the animals, the trees, the seasons. Try chanting: "The earth does not belong to us. We belong to the earth."

You and your friends can make up a world-beat chant and song of thanks by chanting these words and playing your drum, rainstick and didgeridoo.

1   *Tip your rainstick back and forth. Stop.*

2   *Blow a drone into your didgeridoo. Stop.*

3   *Play a heartbeat pattern on your drum several times, starting quietly and then getting louder. Stop.*

4   *Shake your rainstick. Stop.*

5   *Say,* **"The Earth does not belong to us."**

6   *Tip your rainstick back and forth. Stop.*

7   *Blow a drone into your didgeridoo. Stop.*

8   *Play a heartbeat pattern on your drum several times, starting quietly and then getting louder. Stop.*

9   *Shake your rainstick. Stop.*

10 *Say,* **"We belong to the Earth."**

11 *Tip your rainstick back and forth. Stop.*

12 *Blow a drone into your didgeridoo. Stop.*

13 *Play a heartbeat pattern on your drum several times, starting quietly and then getting louder. Stop.*

14 *Shake your rainstick. Stop.*

15 *Say,* **"The Earth does not belong to us. We belong to the Earth."**

16 *Play a heartbeat pattern on your drum several times, starting quietly and then getting louder. Stop.*

17 *Blow a drone into your didgeridoo. Stop.*

18 *Tip your rainstick back and forth. Stop.*

Jabbin Jabbin

"Jabbin Jabbin" was sung by Australian aborigines around a campfire. For over 40 000 years their people have lived in harmony with nature. Sing "Jabbin Jabbin" and notice the pulsing sensation of the song. You can blow the didgeridoo to set up a drone for the song and use the stamping sticks to keep a pulsing beat.

1. Jab - bin Jab - bin Kir - roo Ka —
2. All the birds are cal - ling, rise, —

Kur - ra Kur - ra Kir - roo ka —
Op - en wide your sleep - y eyes, —

Jab - bin Jab - bin Kir - roo Ka. —
All the birds are cal - ling rise. —

INDEX OF SONGS

* TITLES

* FIRST LINES

GLOSSARY OF MUSIC TERMS

A cappella

Music sung without the accompaniment of musical instruments. In Italian, a cappella means "in the style of the chapel."

Accented beats

These are the beats in a rhythm pattern that are stronger because they are emphasized, or stressed.

Aerophone

An instrument that produces sound by making air vibrate, such as a flute or a bull roarer.

Amplify

To make a sound stronger or louder. The hollow body of an instrument amplifies its sound. Your throat and chest amplify the sound of your voice.

Band

A group of musicians, usually playing a particular style of music.

Bar

Beats are organized into small groups or sections called bars (or measures), and each bar has a certain number of beats.

Bar line

A vertical line on a musical staff that divides the beats into small groups or bars.

Beat

A beat is a unit of rhythm in music. A series of beats make a rhythm pattern.

Chant

Words that are spoken or sung in a rhythmic way.

Chord

A series of notes, usually three or more, that are sung or played together to create harmony.

Chordophone

An instrument that produces sound with a vibrating string, such as a piano, a guitar or a bucket bass.

Composer

A person who writes music.

Concussion instrument

An instrument whose parts are crashed together, such as cymbals.

Conductor

A person who leads or directs singers and musicians. The conductor uses a baton to indicate the beats in the bars of music.

Crescendo

A sound that starts quietly and builds to a louder sound.

Croon

To sing sweetly.

Decrescendo

A sound that starts loud then becomes quieter.

Dissonance

A combination of two or more notes that sound unpleasant when played together.

Drone

A steady, constant note.

Falsetto

A low voice that sings in a high head voice. Low sounds come from the chest; higher sounds come from the head.

Harmonics

When one main musical tone is produced, other tones are produced at the same time. They are called harmonics.

Harmony

Two or more notes that are played or sung at the same time.

Idiophone

An instrument in which the sound is made by the vibration of the instrument itself, such as gongs, cymbals or maracas.

Improvise

To make up music as you go, without using songs or scores that are written down or remembered.

Measure

See bar.

Melody

A sequence of higher and lower musical notes that make up a tune.

Membranophone

An instrument that has a stretched skin that vibrates when you hit it.

Note

A musical tone.

Percussion instrument

An instrument that is struck, hit or scraped to produce a sound, such as a frattoire or a drum.

Pitch

How high or low a musical sound is.

Pizzicato

The plucking of the string of a violin, cello or bass fiddle.

Pluck

To pull up or down on a string with your finger, thumb or a pick.

Polyrhythm

More than one rhythm pattern played at the same time.

Resonate

When you pluck a guitar string, the string's vibrations make the body of the guitar resonate, or set up more vibrations, and that makes the vibrations of the guitar string sound louder.

Resonator

The body of an instrument, such as a guitar or a drum, that makes the vibrations of strings, drumheads or air sound louder. Your chest and throat are your voice resonators.

Rhythm

Rhythm is made up of a series of beats. It makes the music flow.

Score

A musical composition that is written down and includes all the parts for instruments and voices.

Solo

A piece of music sung or played by one person.

Sound Wave

When something vibrates, or moves quickly back and forth, it causes molecules in the air to move, creating sounds that move in waves to your ear.

Speed

See tempo.

Stressed beats

See accented beats.

Strum

To play long strokes across all the strings of a string instrument at the same time with your thumb, fingers or a pick.

Syncopated rhythm

A rhythm pattern that upsets the normal way of accenting, or stressing, beats in a bar. Instead of accenting beats 1 and 3, for example, a syncopated rhythm accents beats 2 and 4.

Tempo

How fast or slow the music is sung or played.

Tone

The tone is the quality of the musical sound: soft or harsh, smooth or rough.

Tremolo

Tremolo is a rapidly repeated note, which can be sung or played on the violin, piano or steel drum.

Unison

Two or more musicians playing or singing the same note at the same time.

Vibrato

A wavy vocal sound.

Volume

How loud or quiet a sound is.

Guitar Chords

The numbers on the charts below indicate the fingering. An empty circle indicates optional fingering. A broken line indicates that a string should not be played; a solid line with no fingering indicates that a string should be played open.

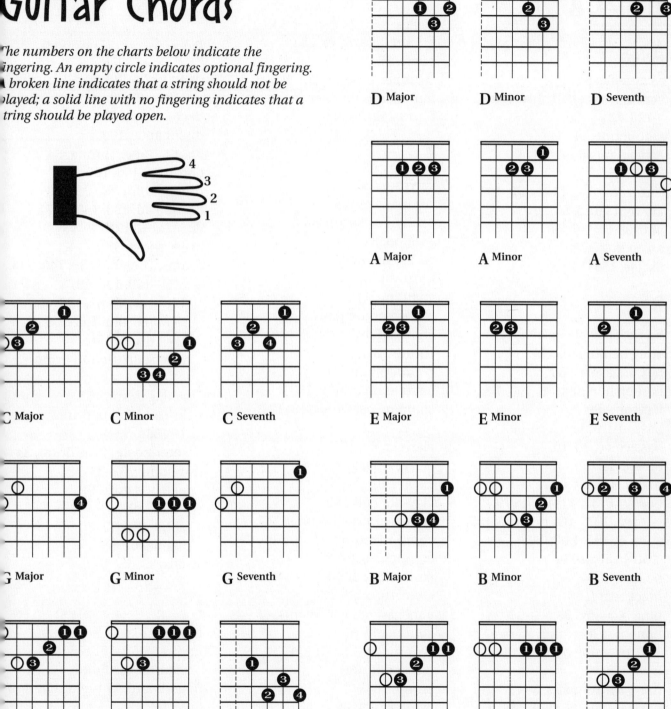

INDEX